THE SCOTTISH COOK BOOK

THE SCOTTISH COOK BOOK

by Sheila Macrae
edited by Mary Norwak

LONDON
W FOULSHAM & CO LTD
New York   Toronto   Cape Town   Sydney

W. Foulsham & Co Ltd
Yeovil Road, Slough, Berks, England

ISBN 0-572-01012-5

Photoset and printed in Hong Kong.

CONTENTS

Introduction			7
Chapter One	North West Highlands		9
	Two	Grampians	25
	Three	West Coast	39
	Four	Islands	51
	Five	East Coast and Central Lowlands	63
	Six	Borders	79
Weights and Measures			93
Index			94

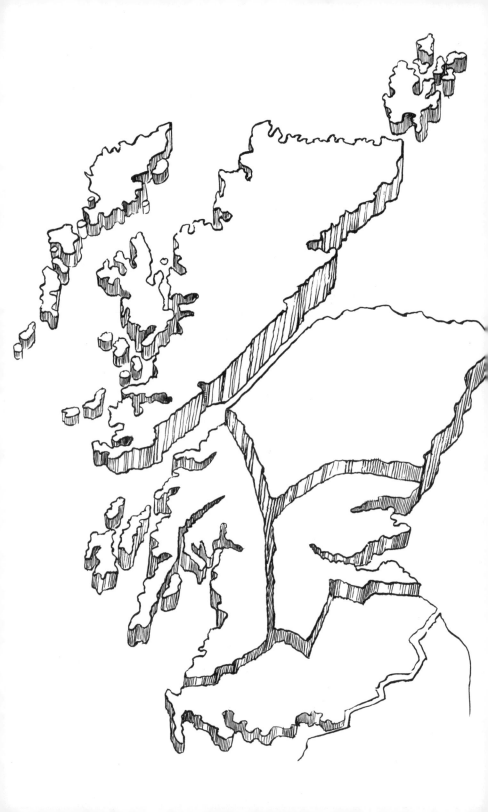

INTRODUCTION

The Scottish cook has come a long way since the days of a peat fire in the croft. As they do everywhere else, tinned foods and ready-made meals make life easier. Perhaps it is this very progress that lends the 'old ways' a nostalgic magic and the determination by many a Scot not to see our recipe heritage bypassed. I've yet to meet a Gran who doesn't enjoy making the old-fashioned Clootie Dumpling, nor a bairn who doesn't love to eat it! I hope that this book will play its part in reviving those special dishes of childhood and help to link hands with Scots the world over.

I have attempted the impossible and divided Scotland into six culinary regions to help our visitors identify with any particular area and its specialities. For some of the more traditional dishes, it was difficult to trace their origins. The more popular favourites such as Stovies and Black Bun are well-established over the whole of the country and some overlaps are inevitable.

Those who understand Scotland know it is a country with wonderful supplies of first class game and the best beef and sweetest honey in the world. It has fruit, cereals and fish enough to give any creative cook a goldmine of ideas. The basic theme running through so many of Scotland's recipes is that of down-to-earth, nourishing and wholesome foods, and the Scots cook's baking is second to none. With their tendency to lead an outdoor life and the need for warmth in an unpredictable climate, the Scots know that these homely meals make sense. Try the mouthwatering Cock-a-leekie soup on a winter's day and you'll understand!

The canny Scots cook is thriving in today's budget-conscious times. Through the ages she has learnt to make a good meal from the minimum of ingredients. She introduced the world to Porridge and there's no better example of cheap nourishment. Hints and tips have been passed from mother to daughter for generations and hopefully this will continue.

Scots the world over have a wonderful and unmistakable fraternity that is celebrated on Burns Night (January 25) and on St Andrew's Night (November 30). On such occasions our old friend the Haggis is responsible for many a patriotic nostalgic tear. Though perhaps not the daintiest of dishes, it is certainly the most symbolic.

Some of these recipes are fun, some economical, and some exciting but each one is a little part of Scotland to create in your own home. These lines from our immortal Selkirk Grace say it all:

> Some hae meat that canna eat,
> And some wad eat that want it;
> But we hae meat, and we can eat,
> And sae the Lord be thankit.

NORTH WEST HIGHLANDS

This is a spectacular land, steeped in history and legends. Everything about it has a tale to tell for here you can find some of the oldest mountains and the wisest people. Its most famous inhabitant has to be our elusive Loch Ness monster – and there isn't a true Scot who doesn't believe in her! Bonnie Prince Charlie made Inverness his army headquarters and it was near here that he lost some 1200 men on the tragic field of Culloden.

The highlands are the majestic homes of the deer, the haggis and the hardy Scot. With the harsh winters, it is not surprising that local recipes are substantial yet, when properly cooked, full of nourishment. Its venison dishes are second to none and the mouthwatering Scotch Broth is a well-established favourite. The bond between kith and kin is important to the Highlanders and their large family meals form an important part of the day.

Porridge

	Imperial	Metric	American
Per Person:			
Water	*1 pint*	*500 ml*	*2½ cups*
Medium oatmeal	*2 tbsp*	*2 tbsp*	*2 tbsp*
Large pinch of salt			

Bring the water to the boil in a large, heavy saucepan. Sprinkle in the oatmeal and salt, stirring with a wooden spoon to prevent lumps. Continue to boil and stir constantly for about 5 minutes or until the oatmeal is absorbing the water. Lower the heat, cover and simmer for at least 30 minutes, stirring frequently. Porridge should be of a good pouring consistency, so add more boiling water whenever necessary.

Note: The making of porridge varies a great deal according to individual preference. Most Scots will sprinkle it with salt before eating. For variety, serve with milk and brown sugar, golden syrup, cream or grated nutmeg.

Some folk find porridge more digestible if the oatmeal is soaked in the water overnight.

Scotch Broth

	Imperial	Metric	American
Mutton	1 lb	450 g	1 lb
Cold water	4 pints	2.25 litres	10 cups
Salt	1 tsp	1 tsp	1 tsp
Pepper	¼ tsp	¼ tsp	¼ tsp
Pearl barley	1 oz	25 g	⅛ cup
Onions	3	3	3
Leeks	3	3	3
Grated carrot	1	1	1
Chopped kail (kale)	4 tbsp	4 tbsp	4 tbsp

Wipe the meat with a clean, damp cloth, then place (without removing the bones) in a large saucepan and add the water, seasonings and barley. Halve and slice the onions and leeks, add to the soup and simmer gently for about 1 hour.

The mutton can be taken out in one piece, if wished, and served as a separate course. It can also be diced and returned to the soup. If serving with the soup, skim the excess grease from the top, add the grated carrot and kail, simmering for a further 10 minutes before serving.

Haggis

	Imperial	Metric	American
Stomach bag of sheep	1	1	1
Sheep's liver	4 oz	100 g	¼ lb
Sheep's heart	1	1	1
Onions	2	2	2
Beef suet	2 oz	50 g	4 tbsp
Salt and black pepper			
Toasted oatmeal	3 oz	75 g	1 cup
Gravy from liver	½ pint	250 ml	1¼ cups

Wash the stomach bag thoroughly, first in cold water, then, scraping, in hot water. Leave to lie overnight in a bowl of cold salted water. Wash again carefully and place in a pan of boiling water to cover, with the windpipe hanging over the side. Add 1 tsp salt and boil for 2 hours. Remove from pan and cut away the windpipe and any gristle.

Clean the liver and heart, washing well, and boil with the onions for about 30 minutes or until tender. When cool, mince the meat and chop the onions. Grate the suet and mix with the meat, onion and seasoning. Add the oatmeal and enough liquor from the meat to make a soft, droppable consistency.

Fill the bag, just over half full, leaving space for the mixture to expand. Sew up the hole with strong thread and cook haggis in a large pan of boiling water for 3 hours. Prick occasionally with a skewer to prevent it from bursting.

Should the haggis be made some time before it is wanted, reheat in boiling water, boiling without the lid for 1½ hours.

Note: There is many a legend connected with the origin and ingredients of the haggis. However, it is – and always will be – Scotland's greatest national dish, piped in with great ceremony at Burns suppers everywhere. It is served with neeps and tatties (turnips and potatoes) and washed down with nips of whisky.

Pan Haggis

Prepare the same ingredients as for the standard sheep's haggis. However, instead of cooking it inside the stomach bag, stew in a covered saucepan for 2 hours, adding more gravy or strong brown stock.

Highlanders

	Imperial	Metric	American
Margarine	4 oz	100 g	½ cup
Caster sugar	2 oz	50 g	¼ cup
Semolina	2 oz	50 g	¼ cup
Plain flour	5 oz	125 g	1¼ cups
Demerara sugar			

Cream the sugar and margarine together, then add the semolina and flour. Knead as shortbread until smooth and then roll into a sausage shape in demerara sugar, coating evenly. Cut into slices and lay on a greased and floured baking sheet or tray. Bake in an oven preheated to 350 °F/180°C/Gas Mark 4, for about 30 minutes. Leave on a wire rack to cool.

Partan Bree

	Imperial	Metric	American
Large boiled crab	1	1	1
Milk	1 pint	500 ml	2½ cups
Rice	3 oz	75 g	6 tbsp
White stock	1 pint	500 ml	2½ cups
Anchovy essence	2 tsp	2 tsp	2 tsp
Single cream	¼ pint	125 ml	½ cup

Remove all the meat from the crab body and set aside the meat from the claws. Boil the rice in the milk until soft and creamy, then stir in the crab meat. Rub through a sieve or pour into a liquidiser until absolutely smooth. Add the stock, stir until boiling, then season to taste and add the anchovy essence. Flake the claw meat and add along with the cream. Re-test the seasoning and reheat, but do not allow to boil.

Highland Hare Cakes

	Imperial	Metric	American
Hare	8 oz	225 g	½ lb
Fat pork	4 oz	100 g	4 tbsp
Stale bread	2 oz	50 g	2 slices
Onion, small	1	1	1
Mushrooms, chopped	1 tbsp	1 tbsp	1 tbsp
Paprika	¼ tsp	¼ tsp	¼ tsp
Egg, beaten	1	1	1
Stale breadcrumbs, as required			

Mince the meats together (or chop finely) and blend thoroughly. Dip the bread in cold water until soft, then squeeze well and mix in with the meat. Chop the onion and fry lightly in butter with the mushrooms and paprika. Bind with the egg and shape into 1½ in/4 cm thick cakes. Coat in breadcrumbs and fry until well-browned.

Note: If liked, top each cake with a pat of butter, creamed with celery salt and black pepper.

Free Kirk Pudding

	Imperial	Metric	American
Plain flour	1 oz	25 g	¼ cup
Breadcrumbs	2 tbsp	2 tbsp	2 tbsp
Farola or Cornstarch	2 tbsp	2 tbsp	2 tbsp
Raisins	1 oz	25 g	2 tbsp
Caster sugar	1 oz	25 g	⅛ cup
Shredded suet	1½ oz	40 g	3 tbsp
Mixed peel	1 tbsp	1 tbsp	1 tbsp
Mixed spice	½ tsp	½ tsp	½ tsp
Bicarbonate of soda	½ tsp	½ tsp	½ tsp
Pinch of salt			
Milk			
Currants	2 oz	50 g	½ cup

Mix all the ingredients together, adding enough milk, gradually, to make a soft mixture. Steam steadily for 2 hours and serve with custard or a hot chocolate sauce.

Roast Venison

	Imperial	Metric	American
Haunch or saddle venison	6 lb	3 kg	6 lb
Butter	1 oz	25 g	⅛ cup
Olive oil	2 tbsp	2 tbsp	2 tbsp
Bacon	½ lb	225 g	8 slices
Salt and black pepper			
Marinade:			
Onion, large	1	1	1
Carrots	2	2	2
Olive oil	4 tbsp	4 tbsp	4 tbsp
Burgundy or claret	1 bottle	1 bottle	1 bottle
Garlic	2 cloves	2 cloves	2 cloves
Bayleaf	1	1	1
Black peppercorns	1 tsp	1 tsp	1 tsp
Rosemary	1 sprig	1 sprig	1 sprig
Sauce:			
Gravy from the venison			
Flour	1 tbsp	1 tbsp	1 tbsp
Butter	1 tbsp	1 tbsp	1 tbsp
Port wine	¼ pint	125 ml	⅝ cup
Rowanberry jelly	1 tbsp	1 tbsp	1 tbsp

Large joints of venison should always be marinated before cooking. For the marinade, slice and peel the onion and carrots, then cook them gently in the oil but do not allow them to brown. Put into a large non-metal dish and add the wine and other marinade ingredients. Soak the venison in this for about 2 days, turning several times a day, so that all the surfaces are coated.

When ready, remove the meat and dry with a clean cloth. Combine the butter and oil in a large, heavy saucepan with a tight lid and, when hot, add the diced bacon. Fry until crisp, then add the joint and brown on all sides. Next, reduce the marinade to half by rapid boiling and strain it over the venison. Season to taste and roast in the oven at 325 °F/160 °C/Gas Mark 3, for 30 minutes per 1 lb/500 g/1 lb.

To make the sauce, strain off the pan juices and reduce them again to half the quantity by boiling rapidly. Rub the flour into the butter and add to the juice. Stir well, then add the port and rowan jelly, blending well. Serve over the venison or in a heated sauceboat.

Traditionally, either braised celery, or a purée of chestnuts is served as an accompaniment.

Hattit Kit

	Imperial	Metric	American
Buttermilk	2 pints	1 litre	5 cups
Fresh milk	1 pint	500 ml	2½ cups
Sugar to taste			
Nutmeg or cinnamon			
Double cream			

Warm the buttermilk slightly. Then add half of the fresh milk, cover and leave to stand for 12 hours. Stir in the remaining milk and leave to stand again until it becomes firmer and gathers a 'hat'. Remove this curd and drain through a hair sieve. Put into a jelly mould and chill for 30 minutes. Turn out, sprinkle with the sugar and spice and serve with the cream.

Civet of Venison

	Imperial	Metric	American
Knob of dripping			
Venison	1½ lb	750 g	1½ lb
Bacon rashers	2	2	2
Seasoned flour			
Plain flour	1 oz	25 g	¼ cup
Wine vinegar	1 tbsp	1 tbsp	1 tbsp
Port wine	1 glass	1 glass	1 glass
Enough stock to cover			
Medium onions, chopped	2	2	2
Black peppercorns	3	3	3
A few chestnuts, if liked			
Mushrooms	2 oz	50 g	½ cup

Melt the dripping in a large flameproof casserole dish. Cut the meat into cubes, dip both the venison and bacon into the seasoned flour and fry until well-browned all over. Drain away all but one tablespoonful of dripping, then mix in the flour and make a brown roux. Add the vinegar, wine and stock then bring to the boil stirring continuously, skim and season to taste. Add meat, onions, peppercorns and chestnuts, then cover with a well-fitting lid and simmer for 2—2½ hours until tender. Add the sliced mushrooms 30 minutes before serving.

Venison Patties

	Imperial	Metric	American
Venison, cooked	8 oz	225 g	½ lb
Salt, black pepper and allspice			
Prunes	4 oz	100 g	¼ lb
Port wine	¼ pint	125 ml	⅝ cup
Strong beef stock	½ pint	250 ml	1¼ cups
Rough puff pastry	8 oz	225 g	½ lb

Finely chop or mince the venison, then season with the salt, pepper and allspice. Stone the prunes and simmer in the port for 10 minutes. Chop the fruit and add to the meat with the stock.

Roll out half of the pastry to line flat patty tins. Spoon in the meat mixture and dampen the edges with water or milk before covering with lids from the remaining pastry. Cut a small hole in the top; then seal and flute the edges. Bake in an oven preheated to 425 °F/220 °C/Gas Mark 7, for 15—20 minutes; then reduce to 375 °F/ 190 °C/Gas Mark 5, for 40 minutes or until pastry is cooked underneath and the filling piping hot.

These patties can be eaten either hot or cold.

Clootie Dumpling

	Imperial	Metric	American
Self-raising flour or flour sifted with 4 tsp baking powder	1 lb	450 g	4 cups
Beef suet (shredded)	4 oz	100 g	1 cup
Pinch of salt			
Mixed spice	2 tsp	2 tsp	2 tsp
Ground ginger	2 tsp	2 tsp	2 tsp
Cinnamon	2 tsp	2 tsp	2 tsp
Sugar	4 oz	100 g	1 cup
Currants	1 lb	450 g	4 cups
Sultanas	1 lb	450 g	4 cups
Semolina	1 oz	25 g	2 tbsp
Egg	1	1	1
Treacle	2 tbsp	2 tbsp	2 tbsp
Golden syrup	1 tbsp	1 tbsp	1 tbsp
Milk	½ pint	250 ml	1 cup
Carrot, grated	1	1	1
Apple, grated	1	1	1

First mix together all the dry ingredients, including the fruit. Add the egg and milk, stirring well to make a soft batter; then add remaining ingredients.

Dip a clean tea towel into boiling water and sink it into a basin large enough to hold the batter. Dredge the towel lightly with flour, pour in the mixture and gather up the cloth. Make sure that the folds of the cloth are evenly distributed, then tie it tightly with string, allowing room for the dumpling to swell. Stand on a plate or saucer in a large saucepan and pour in enough boiling water to cover. Boil steadily for 4 hours, checking the water at intervals.

Turn out carefully on a heated serving dish and dredge with caster sugar. Serve with hot custard.

Scots Trifle

	Imperial	Metric	American
Small sponge cakes	6	6	6
Raspberry jam as required			
Ratafia biscuits	6	6	6
Sherry	¼ pint	125 ml	⅝ cup
Drambuie	2 tbsp	2 tbsp	2 tbsp
Milk	½ pint	250 ml	1¼ cups
Single cream	½ pint	250 ml	1¼ cups
Egg yolks	4	4	4
Caster sugar	1 oz	25 g	⅛ cup
A few drops of almond or ratafia essence			

Split the sponge cakes in half, spread liberally with jam and sandwich together again. Arrange in the base of a large glass dish and sprinkle the roughly chopped ratafias over the top. Pour the Drambuie and sherry over and leave for a while to soak.

Meanwhile, make a custard by heating the milk and cream in the top of a double boiler. Add the egg yolks, sugar and flavouring, stirring with a wooden spoon until the mixture thickens. Pour over the sponges and decorate with whipped cream, glacé cherries and angelica when custard is cold.

Dornoch Dreams

	Imperial	Metric	American
Butter	3 oz	75 g	6 tbsp
Water	1/3 pint	175 ml	7/8 cup
Flour	4 oz	100 g	1 cup
Eggs	3	3	3
Raspberries	12 oz	350 g	3/4 lb
Heather honey	4 oz	100 g	1/3 cup
Double cream	1/2 pint	250 ml	1 1/4 cups
Drambuie	2 tbsp	2 tbsp	2 tbsp

Preheat the oven to 400 °F/200 °C/Gas Mark 6. Place butter in a saucepan with water and heat gently until melted. Remove from heat, stir in the flour and beat well until mixture forms a ball in centre of pan, leaving edges clean. Beat the eggs and add very, very gradually to mixture, beating continuously. Spoon into a large piping bag, fitted with a plain pipe, and squeeze 12 blobs on to a lightly greased baking sheet.

Cook in centre of oven for 20—30 minutes or until golden brown and dry, then leave to cool. Mix the cleaned raspberries with the honey and whip the cream with the Drambuie. Split the buns, fill with the raspberries and cream. Sprinkle with icing sugar and serve immediately.

Fochabers Gingerbread

	Imperial	Metric	American
Butter	8 oz	225 g	1 cup
Caster sugar	4 oz	100 g	½ cup
Treacle	8 oz	225 g	⅔ cup
Eggs	2	2	2
Plain flour	1 lb	450 g	4 cups
Sultanas	4 oz	100 g	1 cup
Currants	4 oz	100 g	1 cup
Ground almonds	3 oz	75 g	¾ cup
Candied peel	3 oz	75 g	⅓ cup
Mixed spices	1 tsp	1 tsp	1 tsp
Ground ginger	1 tsp	1 tsp	1 tsp
Ground cinnamon	½ tsp	½ tsp	½ tsp
Bicarbonate of soda	1 tsp	1 tsp	1 tsp
Beer	½ pint	250 ml	1¼ cups

Cream the butter and sugar together, then add the warmed treacle. Break in the eggs, one at a time, beating well. Sift the flour, fruit and spices into a large basin and stir in the treacle mixture. Dissolve the bicarbonate of soda in the beer and add, mixing well.

Preheat the oven to 300 °F/150 °C/Gas Mark 2. Pour the mixture into one large greased 8 in/20 cm cake tin and bake for 1¾ hours, testing with a metal skewer. Remove from tin and leave to cool on a wire rack. Store in a tightly sealed cake tin. This gingerbread is best left for a day to mature.

Ginger Shortbread

	Imperial	Metric	American
Butter	4 oz	100 g	½ cup
Caster sugar	2 oz	50 g	¼ cup
Plain flour	6 oz	150 g	1½ cups
Pinch of salt			
Ginger Icing:			
Icing sugar	1 oz	25 g	4 tbsp
Butter	2 oz	50 g	¼ cup
Ground ginger	1 tsp	1 tsp	1 tsp
Golden syrup	3 tsp	3 tsp	3 tsp

Sift the flour and salt together into a basin, then gradually rub in the butter until mixture resembles fine breadcrumbs. Mix in the sifted sugar and knead into a smooth ball. Roll out to ½ in/1 cm thick on a floured surface and place in a baking tray lined with greaseproof paper. Crimp the edges with your fingers and prick all over with a fork.

Bake towards the base of an oven preheated to 300 °F/150 °C/Gas Mark 2, for 1 hour or until golden brown. Cool on a wire rack.

To make the icing, heat all the icing ingredients together in a small saucepan and blend well until melted. When smooth, pour over the warm shortbread and cut into slices.

Note: To make the more traditional shortbread, omit the ginger icing. Sprinkle instead with caster sugar while still hot.

Chapter Two

GRAMPIANS

The Grampians are a hunter's paradise and visitors from all over the world come to these heather moors in search of the famous grouse. This important bird tastes its finest when cooked simply and carefully. Roast Grouse has undoubtedly become one of our prime national dishes, served at Scottish reunions for a long, long time.

Proud castles are scattered throughout the area, reminiscent of a warrior people. Many are carefully preserved and one of them, the stately castle at Balmoral, has become the favourite retreat of the Royal family.

Many of the largest clans have their castle seat in these impressive lands and, slowly but surely, the Grampian cooks have revealed the splendid secrets of their ancestors' tables. Each one is a delicacy in itself. They range from Tipsy Lady Cake to Scotch Eggs, and the sheer variety of her recipes does any Grampian cook credit.

Skirlie

	Imperial	Metric	American
Dripping	2 oz	50 g	4 tbsp
Onion	1	1	1
Medium oatmeal	4 oz	100 g	½ cup
Salt and pepper			

Melt the dripping in a heavy frying pan. Chop the onion finely and fry very slowly in the dripping until soft. Add the oatmeal and continue to fry slowly, stirring from time to time until the oatmeal is well cooked, crisp and light brown. Season well and serve hot with chappit tatties and bashed neeps.

Aberdeen Herrings

	Imperial	Metric	American
Herrings	4	4	4
Butter	2½ oz	65 g	⅓ cup
Small onion, finely chopped	1	1	1
Mushrooms, finely chopped	2 oz	50 g	½ cup
Breadcrumbs	2 oz	50 g	¾ cup
Mixed herbs	½ tsp	½ tsp	½ tsp
Lemon juice	½ tsp	½ tsp	½ tsp
Salt and pepper			
Medium oatmeal	1 tbsp	1 tbsp	1 tbsp

Remove the heads, then clean and wash the fish. Split open and remove the backbones.

To make the stuffing: melt 1½ oz/40 g/3 tbsp butter in a pan and fry the onion until tender but not browned. Add the mushrooms and fry gently for a minute. Remove from heat and stir in the bradcrumbs, herbs, lemon juice and seasoning. Divide the stuffing into four, spread one portion on each herring and fold the sides of the fish together again. Place in a shallow, buttered ovenproof dish and brush with the remaining butter, melted. Sprinkle with the oatmeal, cover and bake at 375 °F/190 °C/Gas Mark 5, for about 25 minutes. Remove cover after 20 minutes to allow to brown.

Finnan Haddie Loaf

	Imperial	Metric	American
Finnan haddock	12 oz	350 g	2 cups
Stale breadcrumbs	1½ oz	40 g	½ cup
Butter	2 oz	50 g	¼ cup
Minced parsley	2 tsp	2 tsp	2 tsp
Eggs, beaten	2	2	2
Salt and pepper			
Crushed herbs	1 pinch	1 pinch	1 pinch
Fried mushrooms, minced	1 tbsp	1 tbsp	1 tbsp

Boil and flake the fish; then blend with all the other ingredients. Pack into a greased pudding basin, filling it to within 1 in/2½ cm of the rim. Cover tightly with greaseproof paper and steam for 1 hour. Alternatively, pack into a greased loaf tin, cover with a greased heatproof plate and bake at 375 °F/190 °C/Gas Mark 5, for about 50 minutes or until firm and golden brown. Unmould and serve coated with white sauce mixed with chopped chives.

Cullen Skink

	Imperial	Metric	American
Finnan haddock	1	1	1
Onion	1	1	1
Milk	1 pint	500 ml	2½ cups
Seasoning to taste			
Mashed potato as required			
Butter	1 oz	25 g	⅛ cup

Skin the haddock, then wash and place in a shallow saucepan with just enough boiling water to cover. Peel and chop the onion. Add to the pan and cook until the fish turns creamy. Remove the haddock, separate the bones and flake the flesh. Return the bones to the pan and cook for 1 hour, then strain this stock. Add the flaked fish, milk and seasoning. Bring to the boil and add enough potato to make a creamy consistency. Add the butter gradually and, if liked, stir in 2 tbsp cream.

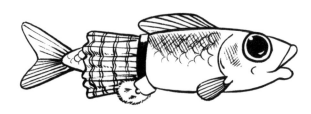

Potted Grouse

	Imperial	Metric	American
Cooked grouse	8 oz	225 g	1½ cups
Butter	3 oz	75 g	⅜ cups
Salt and pepper to taste			
Clove of garlic, crushed	1	1	1
Mixed herbs	1 tsp	1 tsp	1 tsp
Clarified butter as required			

Finely mince the meat twice; then pound until smooth. Gradually knead in a little of the softened butter at a time, seasoning with the salt, pepper, garlic (if liked) and herbs. Press firmly into small pots, making sure that there are no air gaps, and pour over enough of the clarified butter to seal. Chill until set, keep in refrigerator or cool place and eat within 24 hours. Eat with fingers of hot toast.

Pickled Herrings

	Imperial	Metric	American
Herrings	6	6	6
Salt and pepper			
Bay leaves	2	2	2
Black peppercorns	1 tsp	1 tsp	1 tsp
Pickling spice	1 tsp	1 tsp	1 tsp
Malt vinegar	¼ pint	125 ml	⅝ cup
Water	¼ pint	125 ml	⅝ cup
Onion, sliced	1	1	1

First remove the head, tails and fins from fish; then slice along underside and clean, fillet and wash. Dab them dry and season with salt and pepper. Roll up from tail end to head end. Lay the bay leaves in an ovenproof dish and pack the herrings on top. Mix together all the remaining ingredients, pour over the fish and cover. Bake at 350 °F/180 °C/Gas Mark 4, for about 45 minutes or until fish is tender. Leave until cold and serve with a green salad.

Roast Grouse

	Imperial	Metric	American
Young grouse	2	2	2
Salt and pepper			
Butter as required			
Pieces of pork fat or bacon			
Stock	½ pint	250 ml	1¼ cups
Red wine	3 tbsp	3 tbsp	3 tbsp

Truss the birds leaving the heart and lungs inside. Knead pepper and salt into a knob of butter and place inside cavities. Place on a v-shaped wire rack, breasts downwards, in a large roasting pan. Wrap birds in the pork fat or bacon and add more butter to pan. Secure each bird lightly with fine string or cotton. Roast in a hot oven at 425 °F/220 °C/Gas Mark 7 for about 20 minutes, basting 2—3 times during cooking. To test, slide a carving fork into body opening and tip bird slightly until juice runs out. If the juice is very red, cook a little longer. Remove the pork fat or bacon, baste thoroughly, dredge breasts lightly with flour and return to roasting tin without the v-shaped rack. Return to oven for 5 minutes or until well browned. Remove to a heated serving dish and keep warm. Spoon off excess fat from the pan drippings, add stock and wine and bring to the boil for 2 minutes. Season to taste and pour into a gravy boat. Serve the grouse on a bed of lettuce, garnished with watercress.

Scotch Eggs

	Imperial	Metric	American
Eggs	10	10	10
Pork sausage meat	1½ lb	750 g	1½ lb
Salt and pepper			
Pinch of mace			
Crisp breadcrumbs	4 oz	100 g	1½ cups
Deep oil for frying			

Boil 8 of the eggs in boiling water for 10 minutes, then drain, run under the tap and, when cool, shell them. Beat one of the remaining eggs and add one tablespoon cold water. Season the meat and add the mace. Dip the hard-boiled eggs into the beaten egg and cover each one with the sausage meat, pressing it on evenly.

Beat the last egg and gently roll the scotch eggs in it. Dip into the breadcrumbs, pressing the crumbs into the meat. Fry the eggs one at a time in the hot oil until the outside is golden brown.

Scotch eggs can be eaten either hot or cold and are ideal for picnics.

Jugged Hare

	Imperial	Metric	American
Young hare	1	1	1
Seasoned flour	2 oz	50 g	½ cup
Dripping	2 oz	50 g	4 tbsp
Onion	1	1	1
Sliced carrots	2	2	2
Diced turnip	1	1	1
Beef stock	1½ pints	750 ml	3¾ cups
Bouquet garni	1	1	1
Bay leaf	1	1	1
Port wine	¼ pint	125 ml	⅝ cup
Redcurrant jelly	1 tbsp	1 tbsp	1 tbsp

First divide the fresh hare into neat joints, toss in seasoned flour and fry in the dripping until brown all over. Transfer joints to a casserole dish and fry the vegetables in the fat, sprinkling with flour to absorb any excess fat. Add vegetables to the casserole and cover with the stock. Add the herbs and place lid on dish. Place in the centre of an oven heated to 300 °F/150 °C/Gas Mark 2, for 2½—3 hours until tender.

If possible, leave to stand overnight in a refrigerator or cool place for a richer flavour and reheat thoroughly, simmering for about 20 minutes. Place the joints in a heated dish and remove the herbs, skimming before adding the port and redcurrant jelly. Season and thicken gravy, if necessary, with a little flour creamed in cold water and simmer for 2 minutes. Strain over the hare, and serve with forcemeat balls, mashed potatoes, peas and redcurrant jelly.

Note: For forcemeat balls, mix together 4 tbsp breadcrumbs, 2 tbsp chopped suet, 2 tsp chopped parsley, a pinch of powdered herbs and seasoning to taste. Bind with beaten egg and roll into dumplings. Add to stew 15—20 minutes before serving.

Drop Scones

	Imperial	Metric	American
Plain flour	1 lb	450 g	4 cups
Sugar	2 tbsp	2 tbsp	2 tbsp
Baking soda	1 tsp	1 tsp	1 tsp
Cream of tartar	1 tsp	1 tsp	1 tsp
Egg	1	1	1
Buttermilk	1 pint	500 ml	2½ cups

Sift the flour, sugar, baking soda and cream of tartar into a basin. Gradually add the beaten egg and the buttermilk. Beat well with a wooden spoon to aerate the butter. Then lightly grease a hot girdle or large heavy frying pan with suet. Drop on the batter, a spoonful at a time, until girdle or pan is full, taking care that the batter is in neat, round shapes. When scones are covered with bubbles on the top and golden brown underneath, turn and cook on other side. Leave on a clean tea-towel and keep covered until cool. Use remaining batter in the same way.

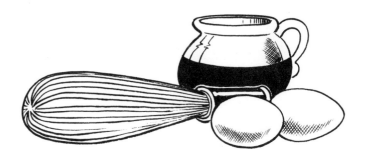

Prince Charlie's Pancakes

	Imperial	Metric	American
Plain flour	4 oz	100 g	1 cup
Pinch of salt			
Eggs, beaten	2	2	2
Milk	½ pint	250 ml	1¼ cups
Large oranges	3	3	3
Large lemons	2	2	2
Butter	3 oz	75 g	⅜ cup
Caster sugar	4 oz	100 g	½ cup
Drambuie	3 tbsp	3 tbsp	3 tbsp

Sieve the flour and salt into a bowl, making a well in the centre. Stir in the eggs and half the milk to make a smooth batter; then beat well and gradually add remaining milk. Melt a small piece of lard in an 8 in/20 cm frying pan, pour in enough batter to cover base of pan and fry until bubbles appear. Turn over and cook other side, then slide on to a tea towel and keep warm. Make 7 more.

Grate rinds from fruit; then squeeze out juice. In the frying pan, melt the butter, stir in the sugar and cook for one minute. Add the rinds, strained juices and bring to the boil. Add the Drambuie and simmer for 3 minutes.

Fold pancakes into quarters and place in the frying pan. Simmer again for 3 minutes, spooning sauce over.

Curly Murly

	Imperial	Metric	American
Fresh yeast	1 oz	25 g	1 oz
Milk	¼ pint	125 ml	⅝ cup
Plain flour	12 oz	350 g	3 cups
Salt	¼ tsp	¼ tsp	¼ tsp
Butter	4 oz	100 g	½ cup
Caster sugar	2 oz	50 g	¼ cup
Small lemon	½	½	½
Candied peel, chopped	4 oz	100 g	½ cup
Eggs, beaten	2	2	2
Icing sugar	4 oz	100 g	⅞ cup
Almonds, chopped	1 oz	25 g	2 tbsp

Dissolve the yeast in the lukewarm milk and leave to stand for 10 minutes. Sieve the flour and salt into a basin and rub in the butter. Stir in the sugar, lemon rind and candied peel, add the eggs and yeast liquid and beat well. Knead on a lightly floured board; then place in a basin, cover with a damp cloth and leave in a warm place until doubled in size.

Divide into three, lightly knead each piece, roll into a 14 in/36 cm sausage and plait (braid) them together. Shape into a wreath, wet the ends and join them together. Place on a baking tray inside a large oiled polythene bag and leave to prove for 20 minutes. Brush with melted butter and bake at 375 °F/190 °C/Gas Mark 5 for about 30 minutes. Cool. Sieve icing sugar into a basin and mix in 1½ tablespoons of the lemon's juice. Trickle over Curly Murly and sprinkle with chopped almonds.

Serve, spread with butter.

Scots Crumpets

	Imperial	Metric	American
Fresh yeast	½ oz	15 g	½ tbsp
Egg, beaten	1	1	1
Flour	1 lb	450 g	4 cups
Salt	½ tsp	½ tsp	½ tsp

Warmed milk, as required

Cream the yeast and stir in the egg. Pour into a large basin and leave in a warm place. Sieve the flour and salt into a basin. Stir ½ pint/300 ml/1¼ cups of warmed milk into the egg mixture and gradually add the flour, beating well until smooth. Add enough tepid milk to give a thickish batter. Cover with a damp tea towel and leave to rise in a warm place for 1½ hours.

Lightly grease a girdle or heavy frying pan with suet. Spoon ½ in/1 cm batter into greased metal pastry cutters and bake until underside is a golden brown. Turn, cook on other side and serve toasted and buttered.

Strawberry Sandwich

	Imperial	Metric	American
Eggs, separated	3	3	3
Sugar	4 oz	100 g	½ cup
Boiling water	1 tbsp	1 tbsp	1 tbsp
Plain flour	3 oz	75 g	¾ cup
Baking powder	1 tsp	1 tsp	1 tsp
Egg white	1	1	1
Heavy cream	¼ pint	125 ml	⅝ cup
Ripe strawberries	4 oz	100 g	1¼ cups
Caster sugar	3 tbsp	3 tbsp	3 tbsp
Vanilla essence			

Whisk three egg whites stiffly; then add one egg yolk and beat for 3 minutes. Add the other egg yolks, again beating for 3 minutes between each addition. Next, add the sugar, water and a little vanilla essence, beating for a further 5 minutes. Sift the flour and baking powder into the basin, and stir in carefully. Preheat the oven to 350 °F/180 °C/Gas Mark 4. Pour the cake mixture into 2 greased and floured round shallow pans and bake in the oven for about 20 minutes. Test with a skewer and, when cooked, turn onto a wire rack to cool.

Make the strawberry filling by first whisking the remaining egg white until stiff, then whipping the cream until thick. Gently fold the cream into the egg white. Mash the strawberries in a basin with the sugar and a dash of vanilla essence. Smooth the filling over one cake and place the other on top.

Tipsy Lady Cake

	Imperial	Metric	American
Madeira or sherry	½ pint	250 ml	1¼ cups
Caster sugar	1 tbsp	1 tbsp	1 tbsp
Squeeze of lemon juice			
Sponge cake layers (8 in/20 cm)	4	4	4
Greengage jam	4 oz	100 g	4 tbsp
Apricot jam	4 oz	100 g	4 tbsp
Raspberry jam	4 oz	100 g	4 tbsp
Egg whites	3	3	3
Caster sugar	4 oz	100 g	½ cup
Blanched almonds, split	2 oz	50 g	4 tbsp

Warm the wine, dissolve in it the sugar and add the lemon juice. Place the sponge cakes on a flat surface and pour the wine mixture over them so that each absorbs an equal amount.

Place one cake on a baking sheet and spread with the greengage jam. Place another on top and spread with the strained apricot jam. Cover with a sponge layer, spread with the raspberry jam and place the remaining sponge on top.

Preheat the oven to 350 °F/180 °C/Gas Mark 4 and whisk the egg whites until frothy but not dry. Beat in the sugar and, when thick and shiny, coat the layered cake with the meringue. Ruffle into small peaks and quickly spike with the almonds. Bake for about 20 minutes until meringue is set. Serve with cream immediately, decorating the base with sugared lemon slices, if liked.

Chapter Three

WEST COAST

The focal city in this land of adventure and progress is Glasgow. Its go-ahead lifestyle and established industries have encouraged its many famous explorers, engineers and soldiers. With its taste for the future, it is hardly surprising that it pioneered the first tea shop and thus became the home of true baking. Shortbread, Baps, Potato Scones and Almond Cakes all have their roots here.

The West is a land of surprising variety. You can be in the centre of a busy oil tanker depot and yet know that countless forest walks are but a short journey away. The beautiful Loch Lomond and the sands of Ayr and Girvin are favourites with holiday makers whilst just a stone's throw inland is a thriving world of factories and farms.

In such a land of contrast, the easy-going people have developed a taste for unusual dishes. Mince Collops and Nettle Kail. Cock-a-leekie Soup and Mutton Pies are firm favourites.

Potato Scones

	Imperial	Metric	American
Cooked potatoes	½ lb	225 g	½ lb
Butter	½ oz	15 g	1 tbsp
Flour	2 oz	50 g	½ cup

Large pinch of salt

Mash the potatoes in a basin with the butter; then beat for a few minutes with a wooden spoon, and add the flour and salt. Roll out very thinly and cut into shapes with a pastry cutter. Bake on a hot girdle or heavy non-stick frying pan, on both sides. Leave to cool on a clean tea towel.

Cock-a-Leekie Soup

	Imperial	Metric	American
Old cock or fowl	1	1	1
Water	4 pints	2 litres	10 cups
Salt	1½ tsp	1½ tsp	1½ tsp
Rice	2 tbsp	2 tbsp	2 tbsp
Leeks	6	6	6

Wash the bird well; truss and place in a large saucepan with the water. Wash the giblets and add with the salt. Bring to the boil, skim and continue to simmer gently for 2 hours. Add the rice and prepared leeks. Cook until the bird's legs are tender (the time involved will depend on its age and size). Remove both bird and giblets, then skim again, adding chopped parsley and seasoning to taste.

Either serve the bird as a separate course, coated with a caper sauce, or chop the meat and return it to the soup.

Note: In some parts of Scotland, cooks add 10—12 soaked prunes about 30 minutes before serving for an unusual, sweet taste.

Hotch Potch

	Imperial	Metric	American
Neck of mutton	1 lb	450 g	1 lb
Water	3 pints	2.5 litres	8 cups
Carrots	3	3	3
Turnips	2	2	2
Cauliflower	½	½	½
Spring onions	4	4	4
Lettuce	½	½	½
Shelled peas	4 oz	100 g	1 cup
Chopped parsley	1 tbsp	1 tbsp	1 tbsp
Sugar	1 tsp	1 tsp	1 tsp

Seasoning to taste

Wash the mutton well and place, with the bones, water and some salt, in a large saucepan. Bring to the boil and skim. Add pepper to taste and leave to simmer for one hour. Dice the carrots and turnips, divide the cauliflower into sprigs, slice the onions and shred the lettuce. Add all the vegetables, except the lettuce and peas, to the pan. Simmer for a further 40 minutes, add the lettuce and peas and cook for 10 minutes. Remove the bones and meat, add the parsley and sugar and adjust the seasonings.

The meat can either be diced and returned to the soup or kept hot and served separately with caper sauce. This is essentially a spring or summer soup, making the most of seasonal produce. Shredded cabbage is often used instead of the lettuce in winter.

Potted Hough

	Imperial	Metric	American
Hough or hock of beef	1 lb	450 g	1 lb
Knuckle of veal	2 lb	1 kg	2 lb
Water	4 pints	2 litres	10 cups
Salt	1 tsp	1 tsp	1 tsp
Mixed spice	½ tsp	½ tsp	½ tsp
Peppercorns	½ tsp	½ tsp	½ tsp

First wipe the meat and cut into pieces, then wash the bone. Pour the water and salt into a large saucepan, add the meat and bone then bring to the boil and simmer for 2—3 hours. Remove meat, add the spices, tied in double muslin and simmer for a further 1½ hours; then strain. Meanwhile, mince the meat and divide between small ramekin dishes. Pour the stock over, stir once and leave to set.

Potted hough is delicious served cold with salad.

Nettle Kail

	Imperial	Metric	American
Chopped nettles	¾ pint	375 ml	2¼ cups
Barley meal	3 oz	75 g	6 tbsp
Butter	2 oz	50 g	¼ cup
Garlic salt	1 tsp	1 tsp	1 tsp
Young cockerel	1	1	1
Water	3 pints	1.75 litres	7½ cups
Seasoning to taste			
Onion	1	1	1

Gather only the tender nettle leaves. Wash them well in salted water, dab dry and chop finely. Measure to exact amount.

Make a stuffing for the bird by kneading 2 oz/ 50 g/4 tbsp barley meal into 1 oz/25 g/2 tbsp of the butter. Add the garlic salt and ground pepper. Stuff and truss the cockerel and place in a large casserole dish or saucepan with the water. Add the remaining barley meal and butter with the seasoning, nettles and sliced onion. Simmer for 1½—2 hours.

Mince Collops

	Imperial	Metric	American
Minced steak	1 lb	450 g	1 lb
Suet	1 oz	25 g	1 tbsp
Onion	1	1	1
Oatmeal	1 tbsp	1 tbsp	1 tbsp
Salt	1 tsp	1 tsp	1 tsp
Stock	½ pint	250 ml	1¼ cups

Brown the meat in a pan with the suet. Add the onion, whole, then stir in the oatmeal and seasoning. Almost cover the meat with the stock and simmer for ¾—1 hour. Remove the onion.

The collops are delicious served on toast, topped with a poached egg. Add tomatoes and curled bacon rashers for a more substantial dish.

Ayrshire Galantine

	Imperial	Metric	American
Ayrshire bacon	12 oz	350 g	¾ lb
Beef steak	12 oz	350 g	¾ lb
Breadcrumbs	6 oz	150 g	2 cups
Salt and ground black pepper			
Grated nutmeg	½ tsp	½ tsp	½ tsp
Ground mace	¼ tsp	¼ tsp	¼ tsp
Eggs, beaten	2	2	2
Stock or water as required			

Trim the meats, removing any skin and gristle; then mince before weighing to the correct weight. Place in a basin and stir in the crumbs, seasoning and spices. Add the eggs and enough stock or water to moisten the mixture. Dip a clean tea towel in boiling water, dust with flour and mould the meat into a roll. Place roll on cloth and sew cloth to fit.

Half fill a large pan with boiling stock or water and simmer the galantine gently for 2 hours. Add some vegetables, if liked, such as carrots, turnips and onions, 30 minutes before end of cooking time. Lay on a large plate and place another on top. Leave overnight with weights to press the meat, remove cloth and glaze before serving.

Mutton Pies

	Imperial	Metric	American
Filling:			
Lean mutton (uncooked)	12 oz	350 g	¾ lb
Salt and black pepper to taste			
Pinch of grated nutmeg			
Mutton gravy or good stock			
Pastry:			
Flour	1 lb	450 g	4 cups
Salt	½ tsp	½ tsp	½ tsp
Beef dripping	4 oz	100 g	½ cup
Water	½ pint	250 ml	1¼ cups

Chop the meat into small pieces, discarding any skin or gristle. Season to taste and add the nutmeg.

Make the pastry by sieving the flour and salt together. Melt the dripping and boil the water. Pour both into the flour and mix well with a wooden spoon to a dough that is cool enough to handle. Knead until smooth. Reserve one fourth of this pastry and keep it warm and covered. Divide the rest into 4 pieces, roll out lightly and use to line 6 small pie tins or large pastry cutters on a baking tray. Fill with the meat, moistened with the gravy or stock, then cut 6 lids from the reserved pastry. Press the edges together and make a hole in the centre of each top, brushing with beaten egg or milk. Bake at 350 °F/180 °C/Gas Mark 4 for 40 minutes. Remove from the pie tins or pastry cutters after 30 minutes and fill the pies through a funnel with the thickened gravy. Serve immediately.

Holiday Bacon

	Imperial	Metric	American
Back bacon joint	4 lb	2 kg	4 lb
Water	2 pts	1 litre	4½ cups
Onion	1	1	1
Cloves	4	4	4
Chopped parsley	1 tbsp	1 tbsp	1 tbsp
Thyme	½ tsp	½ tsp	½ tsp
Rosemary	¼ tsp	¼ tsp	¼ tsp
Carrot, sliced	1	1	1
Peppercorns	10	10	10
Brown sugar	2 tbsp	2 tbsp	2 tbsp
Bacon stock	2 tbsp	2 tbsp	2 tbsp

Leave the bacon joint to soak for 24 hours, or overnight, then drain. Place in a large, heavy saucepan adding the water, onion spiked with the cloves, herbs, carrot and peppercorns. Cover and bring to the boil; then skim and reduce heat to simmer for 1½ hours. Leave to stand until cool. Remove and trim the bacon, rub the sugar into the fatty top and place in a large roasting tin. Preheat the oven to 400 °F/200 °C/Gas Mark 6, sprinkle the joint with liquor from the saucepan and bake for 20 minutes or until lightly browned.

Serve with apple sauce.

Sausage Skirlie-Mirlie

	Imperial	Metric	American
Parsnips	2 lb	1 kg	2 lb
Potatoes	2 lb	1 kg	2 lb
Salt and ground black pepper			
Sausages	1 lb	450 g	1 lb
Bacon fat or butter	4 tbsp	4 tbsp	4 tbsp
Hot milk, if liked			

Peel and cut the parsnips into chunks and boil in enough well-salted water to cover, until tender. Drain through a colander, cover with a clean tea towel, leave to dry thoroughly and then mash. Prepare and cook the potatoes in the same way, mash and add to the turnips. Mix and season well.

Prick and fry the sausages in a little of the fat until crisp and brown, keep warm. Pour the fat from the sausages into a saucepan, add the remaining bacon fat or butter and melt. Stir in the vegetables, whip together over the heat until creamy and add a little hot milk, if liked. Test the seasoning and spoon into a warmed serving dish, arranging the sausages on top.

Stovies

	Imperial	Metric	American
Potatoes	1 lb	450 g	1 lb
Onions	4 oz	100 g	¼ lb
Dripping	8 oz	225 g	1 cup
Salt and freshly ground pepper			
Water	¼ pint	125 ml	⅝ cup

Prepare the vegetables, slicing the potatoes thickly and the onions thinly. Melt the dripping in a strong, thick pan and fry the onion slices lightly. Add the potatoes, season well and pour the water over them. Bring to the boil and leave to simmer gently for approximately 1 hour, stirring occasionally to prevent the vegetables from sticking. Serve hot.

Note: Some folk like to add leftover meat, poultry or game 10—15 minutes before serving.

Helensburgh Toffee

	Imperial	Metric	American
Unsalted butter	2 oz	50 g	¼ cup
Caster sugar	1 lb	450 g	2 cups
Syrup	2 tsp	2 tsp	2 tsp
Small tin condensed milk			
Milk	4 tbsp	4 tbsp	4 tbsp
Vanilla essence	½ tsp	½ tsp	½ tsp

Melt the butter in a thick pan then add the sugar, syrup and both the milks. Let the sugar dissolve completely before bringing to the boil. Heat, stirring gently, to 240 °F/120 °C. Remove from heat then add the vanilla essence and beat well until thick and creamy. Pour into greased tins and mark into squares before it becomes firm.

This toffee has the consistency of a thick fudge when ready.

Paisley Almond Cakes

	Imperial	Metric	American
Butter	3 oz	75 g	³⁄8 cup
Sugar	3 oz	75 g	³⁄8 cup
Cornflour	2 oz	50 g	²⁄3 cup
Rice flour	2 oz	50 g	¹⁄2 cup
Baking powder	1 tsp	1 tsp	1 tsp
Eggs, beaten	2	2	2
Ground almonds	2 tbsp	2 tbsp	2 tbsp
Blanched almonds, halved			

Cream the butter and sugar together in a basin and sift the flours along with the baking powder. Gradually beat the flour and eggs alternately into the butter and finally, when white and creamy, gently fold in the ground almonds.

Preheat the oven to 350 °F/180 °C/Gas Mark 4, and both grease and flour some patty tins. Spoon the mixture to half fill the tins, top each with a sliced almond and bake for about 15 minutes. Leave to cool on a wire rack.

Baps

	Imperial	Metric	American
Plain flour	8 oz	225 g	2 cups
Salt	1 tsp	1 tsp	1 tsp
Lard	1 oz	25 g	¼ cup
Yeast	½ oz	15 g	½ tbsp
Milk	4 tbsp	4 tbsp	4 tbsp
Water	4 tbsp	4 tbsp	4 tbsp

Make sure that all the utensils, as well as the kitchen, are warm before starting.

Sift the flour and salt into a basin and work in the lard. Crumble the yeast into the warm milk and water. Leave it to stand for about 15 minutes; then gradually knead it into the flour. Keep kneading until smooth; then place the bowl in a polythene bag and leave in a warm place until the dough has doubled in bulk in (about one hour).

Turn on to a floured surface and knead again thoroughly. Divide into 6 pieces and shape into flat oval rolls. Place on a greased tray, cover again with polythene and leave in a warm place for a further 15 minutes. Brush with milk and bake in a preheated oven at 425 °F/ 220 °C/Gas Mark 7 for approximately 15 minutes.

If floury baps are preferred, dust with flour before putting into the oven.

Chapter Four

ISLANDS

Around the coast of Scotland there are uncounted islands. Some are large and some small, some are thriving under industrial progress, and others inhabited only by flora and wildlife.

The Island housewife has, through the ages, become an expert in self-sufficiency. The poor soil is carefully tended to yield the widest variety of food and crofting is very much a way of life. A substantial dish can be made from next to nothing – as in Carageen Pudding – and every last piece of meat is used to its fullest advantage.

Life on the Islands can be extremely tough and there is little place for fancy ideals and extravagant foods. Theirs are the down-to-earth, no nonsense meals, perfect for keeping the family warm, healthy and happy.

Potato Soup

	Imperial	*Metric*	*American*
Medium sized potatoes	6	6	6
Onions	3	3	3
Water	*1½ pints*	*750 ml*	*3¾ cups*
Butter	*1 oz*	*25 g*	*⅛ cup*

Firstly, peel the potatoes and onions, then dice. Boil slowly in the water until the potato disintegrates. Add seasoning and butter and serve with a sprinkling of grated cheese.

Powsowdie

	Imperial	Metric	American
Sheep's head, prepared and split	1	1	1
Cold water	6 pints	3 litres	15 cups
Pearl barley	2 oz	50 g	¼ cup
Mixed vegetables	1 lb	450 g	1 lb
Chopped onions	2	2	2

First wash the head well and leave the brain to soak in cold water and vinegar to whiten. Leave the head to soak in tepid brine for half an hour, then blanch and rinse it.

Put the head into a large saucepan, cover with the water and boil for an hour. Add the barley, boil for a further 1½ hours, skimming when necessary. Add the diced vegetables and season. Boil for a further hour and, when head is tender, lift it out and serve separately. Sprinkle with parsley and serve hot.

Note: To cook the brains, simmer for 10 minutes, drain and chop. The meat from the head should be sliced and the tongue skinned and sliced. Serve with a parsley sauce.

Haricot Mutton

	Imperial	Metric	American
Thin mutton chops	2 lb	1 kg	2 lb
Butter	1½ oz	40 g	3 tbsp
Carrots, sliced	2	2	2
Small diced turnip	1	1	1
Onions, sliced	2	2	2
Flour	2 tbsp	2 tbsp	2 tbsp
Water	1 pint	500 ml	2½ cups
Salt and pepper to taste			
Tomato ketchup	1 tbsp	1 tbsp	1 tbsp

First trim all the fat from the chops, then melt the butter in a heavy skillet to lightly brown the chops. Remove the chops and keep warm. Add the vegetables to the skillet and allow to soften but not brown. Sprinkle with the flour and gradually stir in the water, being careful not to allow any lumps. When slightly thickened, add the seasoning and chops. Then cover and leave to simmer for 2½ hours (or until chops are cooked through), stirring occasionally. Skim off any fat, then place chops on a heated serving dish. Add ketchup to pan, stir again. Arrange the vegetables around the meat. Cover with the sauce and serve immediately.

Winkle Soup

	Imperial	Metric	American
Winkles	1 pint	500 ml	2½ cups
Fish stock if required			
Medium oatmeal as required			

Put the winkles in a large, heavy saucepan and cover with fresh water. Bring to the boil; then, using a long needle or pin, pick the winkles from their shells. Strain the water in the saucepan through a very fine hair sieve and return it to the pan. Taste and, if too salty, substitute half for fish stock or milk and water. Return to the boil and sprinkle in oatmeal, stirring constantly with a wooden spoon, until the soup is the consistency of a thin gruel. Simmer, stirring occasionally, for about 20 minutes or until the oatmeal is almost cooked. Add the winkles to the soup and cook for a further 10 minutes.

Arran Potato Salad

	Imperial	Metric	American
Medium potatoes	10	10	10
Fresh peas	4 oz	100 g	8 tbsp
Beetroot, diced	4 oz	100 g	8 tbsp
Seasoning to taste			
Chopped parsley	1 tsp	1 tsp	1 tsp
Chopped onion	2 tsp	2 tsp	2 tsp
Salad dressing or cream			

Peel the potatoes and cook, drain and dry all the vegetables. Dice the potatoes and beetroot and, while still warm, turn the vegetables into a large salad bowl. Season to taste and add the parsley and onion. Carefully toss on the salad dressing or salad cream to moisten and garnish with fresh parsley.

Note: Use either Arran Chief potatoes or another waxy variety.

Lambs' Liver Pâté

	Imperial	Metric	American
Lambs' liver	8 oz	225 g	½ lb
Streaky bacon	6 oz	150 g	6 slices
Butter	6 oz	150 g	¾ cup
Onion, medium	1	1	1
Garlic, medium	1	1	1
Bay leaf	1	1	1
Sherry	4 tbsp	4 tbsp	4 tbsp

Salt and freshly ground pepper

Finely chop the meat, then melt all but 1 oz/25 g/2 tbsp butter in a frying pan. Add the meat, chopped onion, garlic and bay leaf. Cover and fry gently for 15 minutes. Remove bay leaf and mince the mixture finely. Add the sherry and seasoning to taste. Beat well and pour into a small dish. Melt the remaining butter and pour over the top to seal the surface. Keep in refrigerator or cool place and eat within 24 hours.

Clapshot

	Imperial	Metric	American
Potatoes	1 lb	450 g	1 lb
Turnips	1 lb	450 g	1 lb
Small onion	1	1	1
Dripping or butter			
Salt, ground pepper and chives			

Prepare the vegetables. Boil, drain and dry the potatoes and turnips. Chop the onion and fry until clear in the dripping or butter. Mash together the potatoes and turnips, add to pan with onion, stir well and heat through. Season well, including the chives if liked. Serve hot with a knob of butter and garnish with parsley.

Cheese Charlotte

	Imperial	Metric	American
Breadcrumbs	2 tbsp	2 tbsp	2 tbsp
Buttered bread, white	6 slices	6 slices	6 slices
Scottish cheddar, grated	6 oz	150 g	1½ cups
Seasoning			
Eggs	2	2	2
Milk	¾ pint	375 ml	1½ cups

Grease a charlotte mould and coat with breadcrumbs. Remove crusts from the bread and place a layer of the bread and butter in base of mould. Sprinkle a layer of cheese over the bread and season. Continue thus, ending with a layer of cheese. Beat the eggs and milk together and gradually pour into the mould, letting it be absorbed. Leave for 10 minutes. Then bake at 375 °F/ 190 °C/Gas Mark 5, for 20—30 minutes. Turn out when cool, garnish with cucumber and tomatoes and serve with a green salad.

Carageen Pudding

	Imperial	Metric	American
Carageen	½ oz	15 g	1 tbsp
Milk	1½ pints	750 ml	3¾ cups
Lemon	1	1	1
Sugar	1 oz	25 g	⅛ cup

Wash the carageen and soak in cold water for 10 minutes, then drain. Warm the milk, with lemon rind, sugar and a pinch of salt, then add the carageen. Simmer gently for about 20 minutes until thick. It should set to a jelly when tested on a cold plate. Strain into a rinsed china mould and leave in a cool place to set. Unmould and serve with cream.

Note: Carageen is a type of sea moss and can be bought in packets at some chemists and delicatessens.

Orkney Cheese

	Imperial	Metric	American
Rich milk	8 pints	4.5 litres	20 cups
Rennet	½ tsp	½ tsp	½ tsp
Cold water			
Salt			

Heat the milk to 85 °F/30 °C and add the rennet mixed with a little water. Remove from the heat and stir constantly with a wooden spoon for 5 minutes. Leave to stand for 30 minutes to form a firm curd. With a long knife, slice the curd across haphazardly and leave to stand for a further 15 minutes. Stir and strain through a cheese cloth, retaining the curd. Season with salt, gather up the cloth and ease into a cheese cog, or soufflé dish arranging the cloth smoothly over the top. Cover with the lid or a plate and a 7 lb/3.5 kg/7 lb weight. Every 24 hours, remove the cheese and change the cloth. Turn the cheese over and add more weight. Remove after 8 days and leave to dry in a cool, airy place.

Crofter's Plum Pudding

	Imperial	Metric	American
Sultanas	4 oz	100 g	1 cup
Raisins	4 oz	100 g	1 cup
Suet	8 oz	225 g	2 cups
Flour	12 oz	350 g	3 cups
Ground cinnamon, optional	1 tsp	1 tsp	1 tsp
Ground mace, optional	¼ tsp	¼ tsp	¼ tsp
Breadcrumbs	4 oz	100 g	1 cup
Sugar	6 oz	150 g	¾ cup
Eggs, beaten	1 or 2	1 or 2	1 or 2
Bicarbonate of soda	1 tsp	1 tsp	1 tsp
Ale as required			

First clean the fruit and stone the raisins, then shred and chop the suet finely. Sift the flour and spices into a large basin and add the breadcrumbs, sugar, fruit and suet. Add enough beaten egg and ale to make a soft dough, then add the soda, dissolved in a spoonful of the ale.

Bring a large saucepan of water to the boil and dip in a clean pudding cloth or tea towel. Wring out, flour it well and turn the batter into it. Tie securely, leaving space for pudding to expand, and boil for 2½—3½ hours. Alternatively, steam in a well greased pudding basin for 3—4 hours, testing with a skewer.

Note: This pudding does not need the spices if made with the distinctive, original Orkney home-brewed ale.

Bara Brith

	Imperial	Metric	American
Raisins	8 oz	225 g	2 cups
Currants	8 oz	225 g	2 cups
Sultanas	8 oz	225 g	2 cups
Caster sugar	8 oz	225 g	2 cups
Fresh yeast	¾ oz	18 g	¾ tbsp
Milk	¾ pint	375 ml	2 cups
Strong white flour	3 lb	1.5 kg	12 cups
Tepid water	¾ pint	375 ml	2 cups
Lard	8 oz	225 g	1 cup
Candied peel, minced	2 oz	50 g	¼ cup
Mixed spice	1 tbsp	1 tbsp	1 tbsp
Standard eggs	3	3	3

Put the dried fruit in a large sieve, dredge lightly with flour and shake well. Place one teaspoonful of the sugar in a small heated basin. Crumble in the yeast and stir until liquefied. Heat milk until tepid, stir into the yeast and cover. Stand in a warm place until the mixture rises to top of basin.

Sift the flour into a large heated basin, make a hollow in the centre and pour in the yeast mixture. Gradually draw in the flour and add the water. Cover and stand in a warm place, out of draughts, until doubled in size.

Melt the lard slowly, only allowing it to become tepid, then beat into the dough. Gradually add the remaining sugar, fruit, peel, then the spice. Beat in the eggs, one at a time and, when thoroughly blended, divide in two. Knead each portion thoroughly on a lightly-floured board, then place each in a greased 2 lb/1 kg loaf tin.

Cover and leave again to stand in a warm place until well risen in about 30 minutes. Bake in the centre of the oven at 375 °F/190 °C/Gas Mark 5 for about 45 minutes.

Serve, spread with butter.

Cloth Dumpling

	Imperial	Metric	American
Plain flour	2 oz	50 g	½ cup
Slice of white bread, crumbed	½	½	½
Sugar	1 oz	25 g	⅛ cup
Currants	3 tbsp	3 tbsp	3 tbsp
Seedless raisins	3 tbsp	3 tbsp	3 tbsp
Apple, grated	1	1	1
Mixed spice	1 tsp	1 tsp	1 tsp
Syrup	1 tsp	1 tsp	1 tsp
Baking soda	¾ tsp	¾ tsp	¾ tsp
Shredded suet	1½ oz	40 g	3 tbsp
Buttermilk	½ pint	250 ml	1¼ cups

Put all the dry ingredients, with the fruit, into a bowl and add the warmed syrup. Pour in enough milk to make a soft, moist mixture. Turn into a clean, floured and dampened tea towel. Tie the ends together firmly, leaving a small space to allow dumpling to expand. Place in a large saucepan of boiling water and boil very quickly for the first 30 minutes, then simmer for a further 2 hours. The dumpling should be served hot with custard sauce, laced with brandy or sherry. When cold, it may be fried in butter.

Broonie

	Imperial	Metric	American
Plain flour	4 oz	100 g	1 cup
Medium oatmeal	4 oz	100 g	½ cup
Butter	2 oz	50 g	¼ cup
Brown sugar	3 oz	75 g	⅜ cup
Ground ginger	2 tsp	2 tsp	2 tsp
Bicarbonate of soda	1½ tsp	1½ tsp	1½ tsp
Treacle	2 tbsp	2 tbsp	2 tbsp
Egg	1	1	1

Buttermilk as required

Sieve the flour into a basin and add the oatmeal. Rub in the sugar, butter, ginger and bicarbonate of soda. Warm the treacle and add with the egg and enough buttermilk to give the batter a pouring consistency. Grease a 6 in/15 cm square baking tin and dust with flour. Pour in the mixture and bake in the centre of a preheated oven at 325 °F/160 °C/Gas Mark 3, for 1—1½ hours. Test with a warm skewer. When cooked, turn out and leave to cool on a wire rack.

Chapter Five

EAST COAST AND CENTRAL LOWLANDS

Bygone Kings and Queens vied for fame, and beautiful castles and palaces abound in this, the home of Scottish culture. Mary Queen of Scots, for one, is associated with nearly every historic castle from Falkland to Tantallon. Her life at Holyrood in Edinburgh makes a colourful chapter in any history book, a thrilling mixture of romance, mystery and murder.

Here is a sportsman's dream, for Eastern Scotland boasts the greatest golf courses in Britain, if not in Europe, such as Gleneagles in Perthshire and the Royal and Ancient at St Andrews. Fife alone has over thirty courses.

With this awe-inspiring heritage reflected in local fare, some very distinctive dishes have resulted. Forfar Bridies and Kingdom of Fife Pie are amongst the tastiest meat pies in the world, and Arbroath Smokies are a must for every visitor.

Mussel Brose

	Imperial	Metric	American
Mussels	2—3 qt	60	60
Water	½ pint	250 ml	1¼ cups
Fine oatmeal	2 tbsp	2 tbsp	2 tbsp
Milk	1 pint	500 ml	2½ cups

Wash and scrub the mussels well, discarding any that are open. Rinse them several times to remove the sand and grit; then place into a large saucepan and heat with the water. Cover until they open. Strain the liquor into a basin and beard the mussels, removing them from their shells.

Lightly toast the oatmeal and reserve. Heat up the mussel juice, season to taste and add the mussels but do not let them boil. Put the oatmeal into a large bowl and add ½ pint/250 ml/1¼ cups of the boiling stock. Stir it quickly so that it forms small knots like dumplings. Add to the soup and serve hot.

Smokies

To cook Arbroath Smokies correctly, remove the head and tail. Slip into a large frying pan with no more than ½ in/1 cm water in it. Slowly bring to the boil, keeping the pan covered. Cook until heated through; then drain and serve with pats of butter and slices of lemon.

Note: The actual method of smoking these fish is a closely kept secret, known only to a few, but this is an excellent method of cooking them and also applies to other smoked fish such as mackerel.

Forth Lobster

	Imperial	Metric	American
Cooked lobster	1 × 2 lb	1 × 1 kg	1 × 2 lb
Butter	3 oz	75 g	⅜ cup
Flour	1 oz	25 g	¼ cup
Milk	½ pint	250 ml	1¼ cups
Egg yolks	2	2	2
Cream	¼ pint	125 ml	⅝ cup
Drambuie	2 tbsp	2 tbsp	2 tbsp
Chopped parsley	1 tbsp	1 tbsp	1 tbsp

Halve the lobster lengthwise and scoop out the meat. Cut the meat into small pieces and set aside, keeping the shells warm. Make a white sauce with 1 oz/25 g/⅛ cup of the butter along with the milk and flour. Blend the yolks with the cream and add to the sauce. Do not allow to boil or sauce will curdle, but keep warm.

Melt remaining butter in a frying pan, toss in the lobster meat and add the Drambuie. Mix in the sauce and fresh parsley. Scoop back into shells and serve hot.
Note: 1 lobster weighing 2 lb (whole) is sufficient for 2 persons.

Kingdom of Fife Pie

	Imperial	Metric	American
Rabbit, large	1	1	1
Pickled pork	12 oz	350 g	¾ lb
Grated nutmeg, salt and pepper			
Hardboiled eggs	2	2	2
White wine (optional)	3 tbsp	3 tbsp	3 tbsp
Rough puff pastry			
Forcemeat Balls:			
Breadcrumbs	4 tbsp	4 tbsp	4 tbsp
Chopped bacon	1 oz	25 g	1 tbsp
Seasoning and powdered herbs			
Chopped parsley	1 tsp	1 tsp	1 tsp
Egg, beaten	1	1	1

Skin the rabbit, cut into joints and cover with cold water for one hour. Make a good stock from the forelegs, ribs and head. Cut the pork into slices and arrange with the rabbit joints, nutmeg and seasoning in a piedish. Cut the eggs into quarters and place in dish with the meat.

Make the forcemeat balls by mixing together the breadcrumbs, bacon, seasoning, herbs and parsley. Bind with the beaten egg and roll into little balls. Place the forcemeat in the piedish and pour over enough gravy and wine to make the dish two-thirds full. Cover with traditional rough pastry and make 3 holes in the pastry to allow steam to escape.

Bake at 425 °F/220 °C/Gas Mark 7 for 15 minutes; then reduce to 325 °F/160 °C/Gas Mark 3, cooking for a further 1½—2 hours. If pastry browns too much, cover with greaseproof paper. Brush with milk or beaten egg to glaze 10 minutes before serving and, if necessary, fill the dish with more of the gravy.

Musselburgh Pie

	Imperial	Metric	American
Minute steak	1 lb	450 g	1 lb
Oysters	12	12	12
Shallot	1	1	1
Bacon fat as required			
Flour	1 oz	25 g	¼ cup
Salt and black pepper			
White stock	⅓ pint	175 ml	⅞ cup
Rough puff pastry	8 oz	225 g	½ lb

Beat the steak and cut into thin strips as wide as the oysters. Beard the oysters, halve them, dot each half with bacon fat. Slice the shallot, place a slice between the halves, sandwich together and wrap in a strip of the meat.

Sieve the flour into a small basin and add the seasoning. Dip each meat roll in the flour and pack into a pie dish with a china funnel. Add the stock. Roll out the pastry and use to cover the pie. Trim and flute the edges then brush with milk or beaten egg. Cook at 400 °F/ 200 °C/Gas Mark 6, for 15 minutes then lower to 350 °F/180 °C/Gas Mark 4, for 1¼ hours.

Wild Duck with Port

	Imperial	Metric	American
Wild duck	2	2	2
Streaky bacon rashers	6	6	6
Butter	1 oz	25 g	⅛ cup
Salt, cayenne pepper and black pepper			
Port wine	8 tbsp	8 tbsp	8 tbsp
Lemon	1	1	1
Mushroom ketchup	1 tbsp	1 tbsp	1 tbsp
Orange marmalade	2 tbsp	2 tbsp	2 tbsp

Cover the breasts with the bacon and place in a large roasting tin with the butter. Cook for about 35 minutes at 350 °F/180 °C/Gas Mark 4. Before serving, the bacon should be removed and the breasts scored along the breastbone 2 or 3 times, then sprinkled with the seasonings. Pour over the port and the juice from the lemon and return to the oven for 5 minutes.

Keep the birds warm while making the sauce. To do this, blend the pan juices over heat with the mushroom ketchup and marmalade. If liked, the birds can be flambéed; pour two tablespoons of warmed brandy over them and set them alight at the table. The gravy should be served separately.

Note: Wild duck should be hung for about a week before cooking, until a greenish tinge appears on the thin skin of the belly.

Forfar Bridies

	Imperial	Metric	American
Topside or rump steak	1 lb	450 g	1 lb
Pastry	1 lb	450 g	1 lb
Shredded suet	3 oz	75 g	¾ cup
Onion, minced	2 tbsp	2 tbsp	2 tbsp

Beat the meat well with a rolling pin then cut into strips and again into 1 in./2.5 cm pieces.

Divide the pastry into 3 or 4 rounds and cover half of each round with the meat, then with a layer of suet followed by a layer of onion. Wet the edges, fold in two and seal and notch the edges together. Make a hole in the top to allow the steam to escape.

Bake at 450 °F/230 °C/Gas Mark 8, for about 15 minutes until pastry is set, then lower to 350 °F/ 180 °C/Gas Mark 4. Bake until meat is tender when tested with a skewer (about 1 hour). Serve hot.

Note: Traditionally the pastry is only made of flour, salt and water but this makes a hard, tough casing. Many Scots housewives prefer a shortcrust or suet pastry but this too can become hard. A good alternative is rough puff or flaky pastry.

In some parts of Scotland, the filling is placed in the centre of the pastry and the edges brought over the top before being sealed and notched. If using this method, prick the bridies well with a fork instead of making a hole in the centre.

Dunfillan Pudding

	Imperial	Metric	American
Stewed fruit in season			
Flour	4 oz	100 g	1 cup
Pinch of salt			
Bicarbonate of soda	1 tsp	1 tsp	1 tsp
Cream of tartar	1 tsp	1 tsp	1 tsp
Butter	2 oz	50 g	¼ cup
Caster sugar	2 oz	50 g	¼ cup
Eggs	2	2	2
Milk as required			

Sieve together the flour, salt and raising agents; then cream the butter with the sugar. Beat the eggs into the flour with the butter mixture and enough milk to make a soft batter. Arrange the strained fruit in the base of a large buttered piedish and pour the batter over.

Bake at 350 °F/180 °C/Gas Mark 4, for 30—45 minutes until well-risen and spongy. Serve while still hot.

Crail Pudding

	Imperial	Metric	American
Margarine or butter	2 oz	50 g	¼ cup
Flour	2 oz	50 g	½ cup
Milk	1 pint	500 ml	2½ cups
Caster sugar	1 oz	25 g	⅛ cup
Vanilla essence			
Eggs, separated	2	2	2
Ground cinnamon or nutmeg			

Melt the margarine or butter in a saucepan and stir in the flour. Cook for 2 minutes; then cool for a while and gradually stir in the milk. Keep stirring until free of lumps, return to heat and stir until boiling. Simmer for 10 minutes, add the sugar, essence and egg yolks. Whisk the egg whites stiffly and fold into the mixture. Pour into a greased piedish and bake at 350 °F/180 °C/Gas Mark 4, for 30 minutes. Serve hot, sprinkled with cinnamon or nutmeg.

St. Fillan's Paste

	Imperial	Metric	American
Plain flour	4 oz	100 g	1 cup
Sugar	2 oz	50 g	¼ cup
Cream of tartar	½ tsp	½ tsp	½ tsp
Bicarbonate of soda	¼ tsp	¼ tsp	¼ tsp
Pinch of salt			
Butter	1½ oz	40 g	⅛ cup + 1 tbsp
Eggs	2	2	2
Milk as required			
Stewed fruit e.g. prunes, figs, or apples			

Sieve the dry ingredients together into a basin and rub in the butter. Make a well in the centre and drop in the unbeaten eggs. Mix to a thick batter with a little milk. Cover the base of a piedish with stewed fruit and spoon over the batter. Bake at 350 °F/180 °C/Gas Mark 4, for ½ hour.

If using prunes or figs, be sure to have enough juice to cover fruit or pudding will be too dry.

Holyrood Pudding

	Imperial	Metric	American
Milk	1 pint	500 ml	2½ cups
Caster sugar	3 oz	75 g	⅜ cup
Semolina	2½ oz	65 g	⅓ cup
Ratafia biscuits	2 oz	50 g	2 oz
Butter	1 oz	25 g	⅛ cup
Eggs, separated	3	3	3
Orange marmalade	1 tbsp	1 tbsp	1 tbsp
Almond Sauce:			
Egg	1	1	1
Sugar	1 oz	25 g	⅛ cup
Milk	¼ pint	125 ml	⅝ cup
Ground almonds	1 oz	25 g	¼ cup
Orange flower water	1 tbsp	1 tbsp	1 tbsp

Bring the milk to the boil and stir in the sugar, semolina, crushed biscuits and butter. Simmer for 5 minutes, stirring constanly; then pour into a basin and leave to cool. Beat in the egg yolks, one at a time, add the marmalade and carefully fold in the stiffly beaten egg whites. Pour into a buttered pudding mould and steam for 1¼ hours.

Meanwhile, make the sauce by whisking all the sauce ingredients together. Heat in the top of a double boiler until it thickens and serve with the turned out pudding.

Barley Pudding

	Imperial	Metric	American
Barley	8 oz	225 g	1¼ cups
Water	2 pints	1 litre	5 cups
Currants	3 oz	75 g	⅜ cup
Raisins	2 oz	50 g	½ cup
Pinch of salt			

Cover the barley with the cold water in a heavy saucepan. Bring slowly to the boil and boil for 1½ hours, stirring occasionally. Clean the fruit, add to barley, with the salt, and simmer for a further 30 minutes. Serve with caster sugar and single cream.

Costorphine Cream

	Imperial	Metric	American
Milk	3 pints	1.5 litres	7½ cups
Sugar			
Fresh fruit			
Cream			

Pour 2 pints/1 litre/5 cups of the milk into a large basin. Leave to stand in a warm place until a curd has formed. Mix in the remaining milk and leave overnight, again in a warm place. Beat well with enough sugar to sweeten and serve with the fresh fruit and cream.

Pitcaithly Bannock

	Imperial	Metric	American
Blanched almonds	1 oz	25 g	2 tbsp
Orange or citron peel	1 oz	25 g	⅛ cup
Butter	4 oz	100 g	½ cup
Caster sugar	2 oz	50 g	¼ cup
Flour	8 oz	225 g	2 cups

First peel the almonds and chop them finely, then mix with the finely-chopped peel. Knead the butter and sugar by hand on a wooden surface, then sieve the flour and work it into the butter along with the almonds and peel. Continue to knead until smooth then press into a round cake tin about ½ in/1.25 cm thick, or shape into a mould dusted with rice flour.

Cover a baking tray with non-stick baking parchment and lay the bannock on it. Prick all over with a fork and cook in the centre of the oven at 325 °F/160 °C/ Gas Mark 3 for 45—50 minutes. Sprinkle with caster sugar and leave to cool slightly before placing on a wire rack.

Dundee Cake

	Imperial	Metric	American
Sultanas	8 oz	225 g	2 cups
Currants	8 oz	225 g	2 cups
Mixed peel	3 oz	75 g	½ cup
Butter	6 oz	150 g	¾ cup
Sugar	6 oz	150 g	¾ cup
Small eggs	4	4	4
Ground almonds	1 tbsp	1 tbsp	1 tbsp
Glacé cherries	3 oz	75 g	½ cup

Lemon	½	½	½
Flour, plain	8 oz	225 g	2 cups
Baking powder	1 tsp	1 tsp	1 tsp
Brandy	1 tbsp	1 tbsp	1 tbsp
Blanched split almonds	1 oz	25 g	2 tbsp
Milk	2 tbsp	2 tbsp	2 tbsp

Several hours before making the cake, put the dried fruit and peel into a casserole dish. Cover and heat through in a slow oven for about 20 minutes. Stir occasionally until completely cold before using. Cream the butter well with the sugar. Add the eggs one at a time, alternating with a good sprinkle of flour and beating continuously. Stir in the ground almonds, and add the dried fruits, peel, cherries and lemon rind and juice along with a pinch of salt. Mix the remaining flour with the baking powder, blend into the mixture and finally stir in the brandy. Turn into an 8 in/20 cm cake tin that has been greased and lined with non-stick baking parchment. Cover with foil and bake at 300 °F/150 °C/Gas Mark 2 for about 2½ hours. Half way through cooking time, remove the foil on top and scatter over the split almonds. Test with a skewer before removing from the oven and, five minutes before it is ready, brush the top with milk, boiled with one tablespoon sugar, then return to the oven to finish cooking.

Do not remove from the tin until cold.

Petticoat Tails

	Imperial	Metric	American
Flour	6 oz	150 g	1½ cups
Caraway seeds	½ oz	15 g	½ tbsp
Butter	4 oz	100 g	½ cup
Caster sugar	2 oz	50 g	¼ cup

Mix the flour with the caraway seeds, make a well in the centre and gradually knead in the softened butter with the sugar until bound but not soft and oily. Roll out thinly and cut a cake by running a pastry cutter around a dinner plate inverted on to the paste. Mark another, smaller circle inside it, using a saucer or tumbler as a guide. Do not remove the inner circle, but cut the outer ring into 8 'petticoat tails'. Bake on non-stick baking parchment on a tray in the centre of a preheated oven at 300 °F/150 °C/Gas Mark 2, for about 20—30 minutes or until brown and crisp. When cool, dust with caster or icing sugar and serve on a plate in the shape of the original cake.

Tantallon Cakes

	Imperial	Metric	American
Plain flour	1 lb	450 g	1 lb
Rice flour	1 tbsp	1 tbsp	1 tbsp
Butter	8 oz	225 g	1 cup
Caster sugar	2 oz	50 g	¼ cup

Sift the flour into a basin; set aside one tablespoonful to flour board. Add the rice flour. Rub in the butter until mixture feels like fine breadcrumbs. Mix in the caster sugar. Work together with the hands until it forms a soft ball. Place on a floured board and press, with the hands, to ½ in./1 cm thickness. Cut into small circles and place on a greased baking tray. Bake at 350°F/180 °C/Gas Mark 4 for about 30 minutes or until golden brown. If liked, sprinkle a little caster sugar over when cold.

Dundee Marmalade

	Imperial	Metric	American
Seville oranges	2 lb	1 kg	2 lb
Lemons	2	2	2
Water	8 pints	4.5 litres	20 cups
Preserving sugar	4 lb	2 kg	8 cups

Wash the fruit thoroughly, place in a large saucepan with the water and cover. Simmer until the skins are soft enough to be easily pierced. Cut into small pieces in a basin, saving the juice. Separate the pips and tie loosely in a muslin bag. Add to the juice and boil together for 15 minutes then strain the juice into a preserving pan. Add the sugar and fruit, stir until sugar is completely dissolved, then bring to the boil and boil rapidly, without stirring, to setting point (220 °F/110 °C). Remove any scum, cool slightly and spoon into clean heated jars. Cover immediately.

Queen Mary Tartlets

	Imperial	Metric	American
Pastry:			
Flour	4 oz	100 g	1 cup
Margarine or butter	2½ oz	65 g	¼ cup + 1 tbsp
Sugar	1 tsp	1 tsp	1 tsp
Egg yolk	1	1	1
Pinch of salt			
Filling:			
Caster sugar	2 oz	50 g	¼ cup
Margarine or butter	2 oz	50 g	¼ cup
Egg	1	1	1
Mixed peel	1 oz	25 g	⅛ cup
Sultanas	4 oz	100 g	1 cup

First, make the pastry by sieving the flour and salt into a basin. Rub in the fat until mixture resembles fine breadcrumbs and add the sugar. Mix the egg yolk with 2 teaspoons cold water and blend into pastry. Roll out thinly and cut into circles to line 10—12 tartlet or patty tins.

For the filling, cream together the sugar and fat and then beat in the egg. Add the peel and fruit; then divide mixture between tarts. Bake at 375 °F/190 °C/Gas Mark 5, for 30—35 minutes. Check that pastry is cooked underneath before leaving to cool on a wire rack.

Chapter Six

BORDERS

The sedate Border country is the land of romance and poets. Here a tasteful, leisurely lifestyle with its simple but elegant dishes has evolved from the richness of the soil and the beauty of the rivers.

The Tweed is justifiably famous for its delicious salmon. Like the grouse, it can easily be served with sauces and other garnishes, but the locals prefer it as natural as possible with little to distract from its taste.

Sir Walter Scott, one of our most famous authors, lived on the banks of the Tweed. His impressive stately home, Abbotsford, is not far away from the ruins of Melrose Abbey which has beautiful figure sculptures, unrivalled in the whole of Scotland.

Here the emphasis on farming is very great. The wealthy landowners are renowned for taking care of their workers, making sure that they are well housed and well fed.

Baked Salmon Steaks

Cut salmon into ¾—1 in./1.9—2.5 cm thick steaks, or buy cut steaks.

Make a large foil envelope per steak and butter it well. Seal the open edges carefully to prevent juices from escaping and bake in the centre of oven at 325 °F/160 °C/Gas Mark 3, for 20 minutes.

Serve in its own juice, either hot or cold.

Spiced Salmon

	Imperial	Metric	American
Salmon, fresh	2 lb	1 kg	2 lb
Cayenne pepper	¼ tsp	¼ tsp	¼ tsp
Whole allspice	2 tsp	2 tsp	2 tsp
Cloves	8	8	8
Mace	1 tsp	1 tsp	1 tsp
Salt	4 tsp	4 tsp	4 tsp
Wine vinegar	2½ pints	1¼ litre	5 cups

First poach the salmon in simmering water until cooked and tender. Cut into slices and arrange in a crook or earthen casserole dish. Sprinkle each individual slice with the spices and a little salt. Pour over the vinegar, making sure that the fish is completely covered. Leave to stand for at least 24 hours and pour off any excess liquor into a sauce boat. Serve the salmon and spicy sauce with a varied green salad.

Kail Brose

	Imperial	Metric	American
Oatmeal	2 oz	50 g	⅔ cup
Stock	3 pints	1.5 litres	7½ cups
Green kail (kale)	1 lb	450 g	1 lb

Cook the oatmeal in the stock for 30 minutes, adding the stock gradually and stirring rapidly as you pour until thinned to taste and forming knots. Add the shredded, washed kail and simmer for another 30 minutes. Season to taste and serve with oatcakes.

Note: Once this dish was one of the staple foods of Scotland. It was generally made with water for breakfast and with stock for the eveing meal. There are many variations but this is one of the most popular.

Scotch Woodcock

	Imperial	Metric	American
Butter	5 oz	125 g	⅝ cup
Anchovy fillets	8	8	8
Egg yolks	4	4	4
Cream	5 tbsp	5 tbsp	5 tbsp
Parsley, chopped	1 tbsp	1 tbsp	1 tbsp
Salt and black pepper to taste			
Hot toast	4 slices	4 slices	4 slices

Thoroughly blend 3 oz/75 g/⅜ cup butter with the washed anchovies. Press through a sieve and leave in the refrigerator until required. Melt the remaining butter in the top of a double boiler and add the egg yolks, cream and parsley. Stir with a wooden spoon until it thickens, then season to taste.

Spread the slices of toast with the anchovy butter and pour over the hot sauce.

Bride's Pie

	Imperial	Metric	American
Calves' feet	2	2	2
Mutton suet	1 lb	450 g	1 lb
Cooking apples, pared	1 lb	450 g	1 lb
Stoned raisins	8 oz	225 g	2 cups
Currants	8 oz	225 g	2 cups
Cinnamon	1 tsp	1 tsp	1 tsp
Large piece of grated nutmeg			
Candied citron, chopped	1 oz	25 g	2 tbsp
Lemon peel, chopped	4 tbsp	4 tbsp	4 tbsp
Brandy	1 glass	1 glass	1 glass
Red wine	1 glass	1 glass	1 glass
Seasoning to taste			
Puff pastry			

Boil the calves' feet and, when cooked, remove the meat. Mince the meat, suet and apples separately; then blend together along with the chopped raisins and currants. Mix in the remaining ingredients except the pastry.

Line the base and sides of a greased piedish with two-thirds of the pastry and pour the filling into the pastry case. Roll out the remaining pastry to make a lid. Cover the pie, seal and trim the edges. Brush with milk or beaten egg and bake at 400 °F/200 °C/Gas Mark 6, for 20 minutes. Reduce the heat to 350 °F/180 °C/Gas Mark 4, for a further 30 minutes. If the pastry browns too quickly, cover with greaseproof paper, or non-stick baking parchment.

Note: This pie is served at wedding feasts with a symbolic glass or gold ring concealed in its crust. It is usually decorated with Cupids and hearts made from the leftover pastry. Traditionally the bridesmaid who receives the portion with the hidden ring will be the next to wed.

Galloway Hot Pot

	Imperial	Metric	American
Neck of mutton	2 lb	1 kg	2 lb
Onion, peeled	1	1	1
Potatoes	2 lb	1 kg	2 lb
Sheeps kidneys	3	3	3
Salt and pepper			
Stock or gravy	½ pint	250 ml	1¼ cups
Butter	1 oz	25 g	⅛ cup

Divide meat into cutlets and trim. Put trimmings, short rib bones, and onion into a large saucepan. Make into stock with cold water.

Put a layer of sliced potatoes in the bottom of a casserole dish. Arrange cutlets slightly overlapping on top. Cover with sliced kidneys. Season well and repeat layers, ending with a layer of halved potatoes.

Pour strained stock down the side. Dab with butter, then cover and bake from 2—3 hours at 350 °F/180 °C/Gas Mark 4. Remove cover 30 minutes before serving.

This hot pot may require a little more gravy before serving.

Royal Game Pie

	Imperial	Metric	American
Large pheasant **or**	1	1	1
Halved pigeons	3	3	3
Seasoned flour	1 oz	25 g	¼ cup
Mushrooms, sliced	6 oz	150 g	1½ cups
Large onion, sliced	1	1	1
Streaky bacon, chopped	4 oz	100 g	5 slices
Parsley, chopped	1 tbsp	1 tbsp	1 tbsp
Pinch of mixed herbs			
Stock	¼ pint	125 ml	⅝ cup
Red wine or port	¼ pint	125 ml	⅝ cup
Seasoning			
Puff pastry	8 oz	225 g	½ lb
A little beaten egg			

Joint the game; then toss the pieces in the flour and arrange in a 2½ pint/1.5 litre/5⅝ cups piedish. Add the mushrooms, onion, bacon, parsley and herbs. Pour the stock and wine over then season.

Roll out the pastry and make a lid to fit the pie, sealing it down with a little water. Decorate with pastry leaves and brush with the beaten egg. Bake at 425 °F/ 220 °C/Gas Mark 7, for 20 minutes then reduce to 325 °F/160 °C/Gas Mark 3, for a further 2 hours. If necessary, cover pastry with greaseproof paper or non-stick vegetable parchment to prevent it from burning.

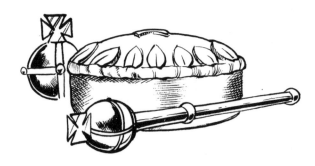

Melrose Pudding

	Imperial	Metric	American
Butter	4 oz	100 g	½ cup
Sugar	4 oz	100 g	½ cup
Plain flour	8 oz	225 g	2 cups
Eggs	2	2	2
Baking powder	1 tsp	1 tsp	1 tsp
Ground almonds	2 oz	50 g	½ cup
Milk	¼ pint	125 ml	⅝ cup
Glacé cherries			
Raisins			

Cream the butter and sugar in a large basin and gradually add the sieved flour and beaten eggs alternately. Add the baking powder with the last spoonful of flour and beat well. Add the almonds and enough of the milk to make a droppable batter.

Grease a mould or basin, and dust with flour and arrange the cherries and raisins decoratively around the base. Pour in the batter and steam for 1½ hours, or until cooked when tested with a skewer.

Leave for a couple of minutes before carefully turning out. Serve hot with a creamy custard or chocolate sauce.

Nettle Haggis

	Imperial	Metric	American
Young nettle tops			
Boiling water	1 pint	500 ml	2½ cups
Bacon rashers	3	3	3
Oatmeal	3 tbsp	3 tbsp	3 tbsp
Salt and pepper			

Use enough nettles to fill a medium-sized saucepan. Wash well, place in saucepan and pour on the boiling water. Bring again to boil and boil quickly, without a lid, for about 10 minutes until very tender. Strain, reserving ½ pint/250 ml/1¼ cups of the water. Chop nettles as you would spinach.

Trim bacon and fry until crisp. Pour the bacon fat over the nettles in saucepan and pour the reserved nettle water into a second saucepan. Bring this pan to the boil and gradually add the oatmeal, stirring constantly. Season well. Lower heat and keep stirring with a wooden spoon until quite thick, then pour into a double boiler or basin over boiling water. Cover and cook for 30 minutes, stirring occasionally. Stir in the nettles, test for seasoning and crumble the bacon over the top.

Grilled Salmon Steaks

For each steak, allow a generous teaspoon of olive oil and a squeeze of lemon juice. Season with salt and freshly ground pepper and leave steaks to stand for 20 minutes on each side in the oil and lemon juice.

Grill under a moderate heat for 20 minutes, turning once.

Serve with a butter or white sauce.

Melrose Creams

	Imperial	Metric	American
Pineapple rings	4	4	4
Large tin apricots	1	1	1
Double cream	½ pint	250 ml	1¼ cups
Glacé cherries	12	12	12
Grated chocolate			

First drain the pineapple rings; then cut each into six equal portions. Rub the apricots through a sieve into a basin. Whisk the cream until fluffy; then stir in the quartered cherries and beat again, gradually adding the apricot purée until it is all blended in with the cream.

Spoon the pineapple equally between six small glass dishes. Spoon the apricot fool over and chill. Top with a thin layer of cream and sprinkle generously with grated chocolate.

Whim-Wham

	Imperial	Metric	American
Flaky pastry	2 oz	50 g	1/8 lb
Cream	1 1/2 pints	750 ml	3 3/4 cups
Caster sugar			
White wine	1/4 pint	125 ml	1/2 cup
Grated lemon peel	1	1	1
Red currant jelly as required			
Candied orange and lemon slices			

Divide the pastry in half and cut into rounds slightly smaller than the diameter of a deep glass dessert dish. Bake on a baking tray lined with greaseproof paper at 450 °F/230 °C/Gas Mark 8 until cooked. Leave to cool; when cold, spread with red currant jelly.

Sweeten the cream with sugar and add the wine and lemon peel. Whisk to a froth and pour one-third into the dessert dish. Cover with a layer of flaky pastry. Repeat these layers, finishing with the cream. Garnish with candied fruit slices.

Oatcakes

	Imperial	Metric	American
Fine oatmeal	8 oz	225 g	1 cup
Pinch of baking soda			
Large pinch of salt			
Boiling water to mix			
Butter	2 tsp	2 tsp	2 tsp

Mix all the dry ingredients in a bowl with enough boiling water to make a stiff consistency. Roll out very thinly using plenty of oatmeal and bake on a girdle or heavy frying pan until one side is cooked. Place in a slow oven until they curl.

Apple Fruit Cake

	Imperial	Metric	American
Apple pulp	½ pint	250 ml	1¼ cup
Sugar	4 oz	100 g	½ cup
Margarine	4 oz	100 g	½ cup
Self-raising flour or flour sifted with 2 tsps baking powder	8 oz	225 g	2 cups
Cinnamon	1 tsp	1 tsp	1 tsp
Ginger, ground	½ tsp	½ tsp	½ tsp
Mixed spice	½ tsp	½ tsp	½ tsp
Sultanas	4 oz	100 g	1 cup
Vinegar	1 tbsp	1 tbsp	1 tbsp

To make the apple pulp, peel and slice the apples. Stew them in a little water with sugar to taste. (A quicker way is to use ready-made apple sauce or apple purée). Rub enough of the stewed apple through a sieve to make required amount and leave to cool. Cream the sugar with the margarine and add all the dry ingredients gradually. Finally add the vinegar and apple pulp, pouring the mixture into a greased and lined cake tin. Bake at 350 °F/ 180 °C/Gas Mark 4, for about 1½ hours, testing with a skewer. Leave to cool on a wire rack.

Black Bun

	Imperial	Metric	American
Shortcrust pastry mix	14 oz	400 g	3½ cups
Stoned raisins	1 lb	450 g	2 cups
Sultanas	8 oz	225 g	2 cups
Currants	8 oz	225 g	2 cups
Mixed peel, chopped	2 oz	50 g	¼ cup
Blanched almonds	4 oz	115 g	1 cup
Plain flour	8 oz	225 g	2 cups
Ground cinnamon	1 tsp	1 tsp	1 tsp
Ground ginger	½ tsp	½ tsp	½ tsp
Ground nutmeg	½ tsp	½ tsp	½ tsp
Mixed spice	½ tsp	½ tsp	½ tsp
Cream of tartar	1 tsp	1 tsp	1 tsp
Bicarbonate of soda	1 tsp	1 tsp	1 tsp
Soft brown sugar	4 oz	100 g	½ cup
Egg, beaten	1	1	1
Whisky	8 tbsp	8 tbsp	8 tbsp
Milk	4 tbsp	4 tbsp	4 tbsp

Beaten egg to glaze

Make up the pastry mix according to packet instructions and roll into a circle 14 in./35 cm in diameter. Use to line an 8 in./20 cm round cake tin, making sure that the pastry comes at least 1 in./2.5 cm above top of sides of tin. Mix together all the remaining ingredients, beating until smooth and pack into the pastry case. Fold the pastry top over to partly enclose the filling but do not push down too far. Roll out the remaining pastry to an 8 in./20 cm round, moisten edges and place lid on bun. Press edges firmly together. Make several holes with a fine skewer through to the base of the cake, then prick the lid all over with a fork. Brush with the beaten egg and bake the centre of an oven at 350 °F/180 °C/Gas Mark 4, for 2½—3 hours or until cooked when tested with a skewer.

Note: Black Bun is traditionally served at New Year and is best made a few months beforehand to allow cake to mature.

Barley Bannocks

	Imperial	Metric	American
Barley meal	8 oz	225 g	2 cups
White flour	2 oz	50 g	½ cup
Large pinch of salt			
Buttermilk	¾ pint	375 ml	2 cups
Bicarbonate of soda	1 tsp	1 tsp	1 tsp

Sieve the barley meal, flour and salt into a bowl. Pour the buttermilk into a jug and stir in the bicarbonate of soda, whisking briskly. When it fizzes up, pour gradually into the flour and knead lightly into a soft dough, handling as little as possible. Roll out gently into a circle ½ in./1 cm thick and cut into large rounds. Place on a hot girdle or frying pan and cook steadily until well risen and brown underneath (about 5 minutes), then turn and brown other side. When edges are dry, they are ready. Alternatively, place on a greased baking tray and brush with milk. Bake for 10—12 minutes at 425 °F/220 °C/Gas Mark 7, and leave to cool on a wire rack.

Selkirk Bannock

	Imperial	Metric	American
Dried yeast	2 tsp	2 tsp	2 tsp
Caster sugar	2½ tsp	2½ tsp	2½ tsp
Warm milk	¼ pint	125 ml	⅝ cup
Egg, beaten	1	1	1
Strong white plain flour	10 oz	300 g	2½ cups
Pinch of salt			
Butter	1 oz	25 g	⅛ cup
Sultanas	1 oz	25 g	¼ cup
Currants	1 oz	25 g	¼ cup
Mixed peel	1 oz	25 g	⅛ cup
Beaten egg to glaze			

Mix the yeast with one teaspoonful of sugar and sprinkle over the warm milk blended in a small basin with the egg. Leave in a warm place for 15 minutes.

Sift the flour, half a teaspoonful of sugar and the salt into a warmed basin; then rub in the butter. Using a wooden spoon, beat the yeast liquid into the flour to form a dough. Add the fruit and peel, knead well and place in an oiled polythene bag. Tie loosely and leave to rise until doubled in size and springy to touch. Knead again until firm.

Shape to fit a 7—8 in./18—20 cm, lightly greased round shallow cake tin. Using a sharp knife, score the top into 8 sections and leave in a warm place to proove until dough reaches top of tin. Brush with beaten egg and bake in a preheated oven at 400 °F/200 °C/Gas Mark 6 for 35 minutes. For a sticky coating, dissolve the remaining sugar in a tablespoonful of water. Brush the bannock with this mixture as soon as it is removed from the oven.

METRICATION

It is very important to use either the imperial table for measuring ingredients *or* the metric one, and not to mix them when preparing a recipe. The metric scale is not an exact translation of the imperial one, which would be very cumbersome, but the recipes have been tested to arrive at the correct proportions. The metric result is approximately 10% less than that gained with imperial measurements.

The metric scale recommended for British use allows 25 g to 1 oz; and 25 ml to 1 fl oz, instead of the true scale of 28 g to 1 oz. This means that quantities must be 'rounded up' at certain points on the scale, or else vital amounts will be lost as total recipe quantities become larger.

Solid Measures

½ oz	15 g
1 oz	25 g
2 oz	50 g
3 oz	75 g
4 oz	100 g
5 oz	125 g
6 oz	150 g
7 oz	175 g
8 oz	225 g
9 oz	250 g
10 oz	300 g
11 oz	325 g
12 oz	350 g
13 oz	375 g
14 oz	400 g
15 oz	425 g
16 oz	450 g or 500 g
1½ lb	750 g
2 lb	1 kg

Liquid Measures

½ fl oz	15 ml
1 fl oz	25 ml
2 fl oz	50 ml
3 fl oz	75 ml
4 fl oz	100 ml
¼ pint	125 ml
⅓ pint	175 ml
½ pint	250 ml
⅔ pint	350 ml
¾ pint	375 ml
1 pint	500 ml
1¼ pints	625 ml
1½ pints	750 ml
1¾—2 pints	1 litre

When meat and vegetables and some groceries are purchased in metric measure, they will normally be in 1 lb or 2 lb measurement equivalents, and people will ask for .5 kg or 1 kg which is 500 g or 1000 g. When baking, a measurement of 450 g is in proportion with the smaller amounts of ingredients needed.

INDEX

Aberdeen Herrings **26**
Apple Fruit Cake **89**
Arran Potato Salad **54**
Ayrshire Galantine **44**

Bacon, Holiday **46**
Baked Salmon Steaks **79**
Bannocks, Barley **91**
  Pitcaithly **75**
  Selkirk **92**
Baps **50**
Bara Brith **60**
Barley Pudding **73**
Black Bun **90**
Bride's Pie **82**
Bridies, Forfar **69**
Broonie **62**
Broth, Scotch **11**

Cake, Apple Fruit **89**
  Dundee **74**
  Fochabers Gingerbread **23**
  Highland Hare **14**
  Paisley Almond **49**
  Strawberry Sandwich **37**
  Tantallon **76**
  Tipsy Lady **38**
Carageen Pudding **57**
Cheese Charlotte **56**
Cheese, Orkney **58**
Civet of Venison **18**
Clapshot **56**
Clootie Dumpling **20**
Cloth Dumpling **61**
Cock-a-Leekie Soup **40**
Costorphine Cream **73**
Crail Pudding **70**
Crofter's Plum Pudding **59**
Crumpets, Scots **36**
Cullen Skink **28**
Curly Murly **35**

Dornoch Dreams **22**
Drop Scones **33**
Dumpling, Clootie **20**
  Cloth **61**
Dundee Cake **74**
  Marmalade **77**
Dunfillan Pudding **70**

Finnan Haddie Loaf **27**

Fochabers Gingerbread **23**
Forfar Bridies **69**
Forth Lobster **65**
Free Kirk Pudding **15**

Galloway Hot Pot **83**
Ginger Shortbread **24**
Grilled Salmon Steaks **87**
Grouse, Potted **28**
  Roast **30**

Haggis **12**
  Nettle **86**
  Pan **13**
Hare, Jugged **32**
Haricot Mutton **53**
Hattit Kit **16**
Helensburgh Toffee **48**
Herrings, Aberdeen **26**
  Pickled **29**
Highlanders **13**
Highland Hare Cakes **14**
Holiday Bacon **46**
Holyrood Pudding **72**
Hotch Potch **41**
Hot Pot, Galloway **83**

Jugged Hare **32**

Kail Brose **80**
Kingdom of Fife Pie **66**

Lambs' Liver Pâté **55**
Lobster, Forth **65**

Marmalade, Dundee **77**
Melrose Creams **87**
  Pudding **85**
Mince Collops **43**
Mussel Brose **64**
Musselburgh Pie **67**
Mutton Pies **45**
Mutton, Haricot **53**

Nettle Haggis **86**
  Kail **42**

Oatcakes **88**
Orkney Cheese **58**

Paisley Almond Cakes **49**
Pancakes, Prince Charlie's **34**

Pan Haggis 13
Partan Bree 14
Pâté, Lambs' Liver 55
Petticoat Tails 76
Pickled Herrings 29
Pie, Bride's 82
  Kingdom of Fife 66
  Musselburgh 67
  Mutton 45
  Royal Game 84
Pitcaithly Bannock 75
Porridge 10
Potato Scones 39
  Soup 51
Potted Grouse 28
  Hough 42
Powsowdie 52
Prince Charlie's Pancakes 34
Pudding Barley 73
  Carageen 57
  Crail 70
  Crofter's Plum 59
  Dunfillan 70
  Free Kirk 15
  Holyrood 72
  Melrose 85

Queen Mary Tartlets 78

Roast Grouse 30
  Venison 16
Royal Game Pie 84

Salad, Arran Potato 54
Salmon, Baked Steaks 79
  Spiced 80
  Grilled Steaks 87
Sausage Skirlie-Mirlie 47

Scones, Drop 33
  Potato 39
Scotch Broth 11
Scoth Eggs 31
Scotch Woodcock 81
Scots Crumpets 36
Scots Trifle 21
Selkirk Bannock 92
Shortbread, Ginger 24
Skirlie 25
Smokies 64
Soups, Cock-a-Leekie 40
  Cullen Skink 28
  Hotch Potch 41
  Kail Brose 80
  Mussel Brose 64
  Partan Bree 14
  Potato 51
  Powsowdie 52
  Scotch Broth 11
  Winkle 54
Spiced Salmon 80
St. Fillan's Paste 71
Stovies 48
Strawberry Sandwich 37

Tantallon Cakes 76
Tipsy Lady Cake 38
Toffee, Helensburgh 48
Trifle, Scots 21

Venison, Civet 18
  Patties 19
  Roast 16

Whim-Wham 88
Wild Duck with Port 68
Winkle Soup 54
Woodcock, Scotch 81